Jataka Tales

Birth Stories of Buddha

Jataka Tales

Birth Stories of Buddha

Retold by
Ethel Beswick

With a foreword by
E. Conze

PILGRIMS PUBLISHING
◆ Varanasi ◆

Jataka Tales
Ethel Beswick

Published by:
BOOK FAITH INDIA

An imprint of:
PILGRIMS BOOK HOUSE (New Delhi)
1626, Raj Guru Road Pahar Ganj, Chuna Mandi
New Delhi 110055
Tel: 91-11-23584015, 23584019
E-mail: pilgrim@del2.vsnl.net.in
E-mail: pilgrimsinde@gmail.com

First Printed in 1936
Copyright © 2007, Pilgrims Publishing
All Rights Reserved

ISBN: 81-7303-173-8

Printed in India at Pilgrim Press Pvt. Ltd. Lalpur Varanasi

CONTENTS

v

EDITORIAL NOTE

THE object of the Editor of this series is a very definite one. He desires above all things that these books shall be the ambassadors of good-will between East and West. He hopes that they will contribute to a fuller knowledge of the great cultural heritage of the East, for only through real understanding will the West be able to appreciate the underlying problems and aspirations of Asia to-day. He is confident that a deeper knowledge of the great ideals and lofty philosophy of Eastern thought will help to a revival of that true spirit of charity which neither despises nor fears the nations of another creed and colour.

J. L. CRANMER-BYNG

50 ALBEMARLE STREET
LONDON W.I

FOREWORD

In their desire to be all things to all men, the Buddhists of India presented the doctrine of the Enlightened One in the form of learned treatises to one kind of public, in the form of delightful tales to another. In the translation of the philosophical treatises a strict, and even pedantic, literalness ought to be observed. This is not so, on the other hand, with the Tales and Fables, which lose most of their charm and flavour in the process. The conventions of Indian story telling are, indeed, so different from our own, that their literal reproduction makes tiresome reading. The six volumes of the Cambridge translation of the Pali version of the Jatakas are of great value to scholars for philological, historical and archaeological purposes. No one, however, would read them for pleasure. In order to be more widely appreciated, the Birth Stories must obviously be retold in the idiom of to-day. This need not, as Miss Beswick's selections demonstrate, involve any distortion of the underlying teachings, and her rendering is alive with the spiritual purpose and message which unknown monks thousands of years ago have infused into the folklore of India.

EDWARD CONZE

INTRODUCTION

THE Jataka Tales (Birth-Stories)—of which there are 547—are tales told by the Buddha of his previous births as bird, animal, man. They were remembered and recorded by his followers not long after his death.

It is not a new idea that some people can recall their past lives on earth (though much so-called memory is wishful thinking or imagination) for Pythagoras, whom no one could accuse of wishful thinking or embroidery, gave instances of a few of his own past lives. And since the main teaching of the Buddha was that actions bring their due effects under immutable law, against which all prayers are unavailing, and that each life is the outcome of previous lives, it is not surprising that part of his method of impressing this on his listeners was by means of the descriptions of the past lives of himself and of others, showing not only the relationship between people but also in graphic form what evil is like and what good qualities are like.

Throughout the stories we see the line of life possessing those spiritual qualities which blossom in Buddhahood acting in and through various types of bodies, always helping, always reasoning, acting after forethought, full of effort and animated by love, finally developing the power to sacrifice life itself. The qualities of friendship are brought out clearly in such delightful stories as the deer, the woodpecker and the tortoise; or in finer form in the actions of Banyan, the golden deer, the great-hearted monkey, and the love of the elephant's wife caught by a crab. Duty is extolled: determination and perseverance are shown as necessary qualities to possess, and the power of evil is shown in all its degradation. It is interesting, by the way, to note that

1

throughout the animal stories there is little or no *evil* in them, but when the stories deal with human beings we see cruelty and evil in abundance !

The stories were told around some incident then happening, and it is in their relationship with that incident that we find their true lesson. At the close of the story the Buddha always identified the birth so that lines of action and character stand out clearly from the past to the present, sometimes the same, sometimes changed for the better.

It is not surprising that his favourite disciple, Ananda, and the two chief members of his Brotherhood, Sariputta and Moggallana, should appear very often with him as his friends of the past, and Devadatta, his cousin who tried often to destroy him in various ways, as his enemy. With poetic licence these sometimes appear as human beings while the life-to-become-the-Buddha was still in animal form, as in the case of the birth as the " Obedient Elephant ", where Ananda was the mahout and Devadatta the evil king.

After the death of the Buddha representations of the stories were carved on stone or painted on rock, as on the gates of the great Sanchi *Stupa* or memorial, the eastern gate of which was taken as one of the archaeological series of stamps by India when attaining her freedom. Also at the Bharhut Stupa and the Ajanta caves.

Much more of the Buddha's teaching can of course be found elsewhere, in *The Dhammapada*,[1] the Footsteps of the Law, a collection of sayings of the Buddha accepted as such at the Council of King Asoka, 240 B.C., and in the voluminous writings that have grown up around the teachings during the centuries.

Who was the Buddha ? Dr. Radhakrishnan in his lecture,

[1] A Selection is published in the Wisdom of the East Series: *The Dhammapada*, trans. by Nārada Thera.

'Gautama the Buddha', 1938 (one of the annual Henriette Hertz Trust lectures on a Master Mind, at the British Academy), said "He belongs to the history of the world's thought, to the general inheritance of all cultivated men; for, judged by intellectual integrity, moral earnestness and spiritual insight, he is undoubtedly one of the greatest figures in history."

As for biographical information about this great Sage, there is no doubt that he was born of a royal family at Kapilavastu in north-east India about 500 B.C. His father was King Suddhodana, his mother Queen Maya. Before he was born, Queen Maya dreamt that a star fell from Heaven and entered her womb, and when the child was born it is said that the rocks gave water for his first bath while the trees made a bower for the queen. He was given the name of Siddharta, which is a shortened form of *Sarvârtthasiddha*—the 'realization of all desires'. His family name was Gautama—'on earth the most victorious'. The story tells of the visit of the 'Wise Men' to see the baby, of the warnings given to the king that his son might not rule the kingdom, of the young boy surprising his tutors with his knowledge, of his play with his cousins and the shooting down of a swan giving the boy his first knowledge of pain. The swan was shot down with an arrow by his cousin Devadatta but Siddharta picked it up and, calming the fluttering bird, removed the arrow. Wondering why the bird should have fallen he pricked his own flesh with the sharp point of the arrow and felt pain for the first time. When his cousin claimed the bird as his by right of conquest, the prince said that it was his, for he had saved its life.

We read of the great tournament held for the hand of beautiful Yasodhara, and of Siddharta's triumph and marriage. We read of the terror of the king lest the young prince should know sorrow or suffering, and of the beautiful palace in which he

lived.   We read of his first journey into the capital of the kingdom and of the king's care that all signs of death or sorrow should
be kept off the streets.   But, as Sir Edwin Arnold says in his
Light of Asia: ' Who shall shut out fate ? '

We read how he met illness, death and sorrow in the city,
of the first dawning in his mind that such things come to all,
even to Yasodhara ; of the cruelty he sensed under the smiling
waters wherein ' life feeds on life '.   How everywhere things
are not what they seem, and, finally, when he left the palace one
night on his faithful horse Kantaka, how the gates opened of
themselves, and no sound of the horses' hoofs was heard.   We
read how he sent his servant and horse back and he himself
wandered off into the forest to live with hermits and yogis
and try to find out the cause of sorrow.   After much effort,
along one line and another of bodily torture, he realized that
this way knowledge would not come to him and, refreshed by
the milk given him by a young mother, he rested under a tree
and meditated on the great problems of life.

We can read, in the magical language of eastern symbology,
how he finally achieved Enlightenment under the Bodhi tree,
and against all the snares of Mara, the prince of evil, was un-
moved.   At the critical moment of his vision he saw the worlds
and all living things in a vast array and himself as one with
them, losing himself in the Bliss that lies at the centre of the
Universe.   That same vast Universe was in suspense lest he
should forsake his fellow men and enter the Bliss, but he
triumphed and obeyed the call of the suffering and said he would
stay and preach the Word.

For forty years he wandered over India teaching the great
truths of life and gathering around himself disciples, the chief
among them being Ananda.   His first sermon was at the deer
park at Sarnath, near Benares, and the text of this sermon has

come down to us, as have many of his sayings, for immediately after his death his disciples gathered together and recorded all they could remember.

Though he says that his own knowledge is as much greater than that which he passed on as are all the leaves of a tree compared to one leaf, yet we have enough to go on in the *Pancha Sila*, or Five Virtues, his Four Noble Truths and the Noble Eightfold Path.

The *Pancha Sila* reminds us of the Old Testament Commandments in some respects:

> Kill not—for Pity's sake—and lest ye slay
> The meanest thing upon its upward way.
>
> Give freely and receive, but take from none
> By greed, or force, or fraud, what is his own.
>
> Bear not false witness, slander not, nor lie;
> Truth is the speech of inward purity.
>
> Shun drugs and drinks which mind and soul abuse;
> Clear minds, clean bodies, need no Soma juice.
>
> Touch not thy neighbour's wife, neither commit
> Sins of the flesh unlawful and unfit.
>
> *Light of Asia*

The Four Noble Truths are Sorrow: all is sorrow; Sorrow's Cause, Sorrow's Ceasing, and the Way.

The Eightfold Path deals with The Way, that Way of Life which all must follow in the end, for we must have Right Doctrine, Right Purpose, Right Speech, Right Behaviour, Right Purity, Right Thought, Right Loneliness and Right Rapture.

He taught the doctrine of Karma, that Law of Cause and Effect,

of sowing and reaping, which makes each man reap the fruits
in life (in some rebirth or other) of his deeds, good or bad, thus
making him master of his fate.   He showed, too, the brotherhood
of all, of man and beast, of star and dewdrop; he taught how
all lives and moves on on the great wheel of time, but that this
wheel can be broken by effort in the right way.   It is said
that never was his voice raised in anger, and indeed, throughout
all his sermons and sayings we find the spirit of love and understanding.   In one story it is said that he offered his begging
bowl at the door of a man who refused him food and grumbled
at him for not working, and abused him.   The Buddha said
to him, " If a man gives a present to another man who refuses
to accept it, to whom does the present belong?"   The man
answered: " To him who offered it."   " Then," said the
Buddha, " if I do not accept your abuse it will return to you.
But I have lost a friend."

He taught till he was eighty years old, and when he was about
to put off his body his last words were: " All compounds are
perishable."

For many years his teachings flourished, and as one writer
put it: ' There was a time, when from the mountains and
plains of the north to the woods and downs of Ceylon, there
was but one rallying cry, to save mankind from the miseries
of ignorance in the name of Him who first taught the Brotherhood of man.'   But here, too, as with all other great missions,
the teachings began to give place to ceremony, then to be forgotten as a way of life.   The orthodoxy of the Brahmins and
Muslim conquest succeeded in driving them out of India to a
great extent, and the Buddhist monks took refuge in Burma
and China as well as in other parts of the world.

But nothing can finally drive out Truth, and again and again
these teachings are revived, put into other words, other symbols,

as they were by Jesus, until, at last, mankind shall learn that
' Hatred ceaseth not by hatred, but by love; this is the LAW .

I have used almost exclusively the six volumes of *The Jataka*,
or Stories of the Buddha's Former Births, translated from the
Pali by various hands under the Editorship of Professor E. B.
Cowell, Cambridge University Press 1895–1897, 1901–1907
(6 volumes), as I do not know Pali.

These volumes are of great value to the scholar but they con-
tain so much: the stories are often of great length, being trans-
lations, and the general reader would, I am afraid, neither wish
to read six volumes nor be interested in many of the stories.
I have therefore picked out those which are, I think, the simplest
and most easily understood, and which have a strong appeal to
the higher qualities of man. In re-telling them I have reduced
many considerably in length and, I hope, still retained the spirit
while simplifying the form of presentation.

The verses quoted at the end of the stories are verbatim from
the Cambridge volumes, though in some cases I have taken only
a few verses for each story.

In these days when horror and evil seem to be our daily food,
it seems good to turn to something which, while not ignor-
ing evil or making goodness effeminate, will still give some
basis of thought truly educative to human beings; something
which will hold up an ideal as a pattern for life, and stretch
our vision, so limited in terms of the various high-powered
bombs, till we can see an infinite vista before us. Not an endless nothingness, or endless misery, not a snuffing-out, but a
life that lives for all time as a power for good, part of that ever-
present, living company of the sages of the past and of the future.

Though hatred can and will cease, love is immortal.

THE FAIRY CANDA

ONE day after his Enlightenment the Buddha was seated with his father, King Suddhodana, taking a meal and he told him a story. After the meal he said he would visit Yasodhara, the mother of his son Rahula, in her house and tell her a story also.

When Yasodhara heard that he was coming she arranged a welcome for him, and when he arrived greeted him with great reverence.

The king then told the Buddha that while he had been searching for Truth, as a beggar, and without possessions, she had cast aside all her jewels and garlands to be like him, and when he had achieved Buddhahood she had also worn the yellow robe—" So faithful is her heart to you ".

The Buddha answered that it was not strange she should love him in this birth and be faithful to him, for she had been so in the past. And he told the following story.

Once the life that was to become the Buddha was born as a fairy and called Canda. He lived with his fairy wife, Candā,[1] in the Himalayas on a silver mountain called Chandapabhata, or Mountain of the Moon.

In the rainy season they remained on the mountain, but in the hot weather after the rains they came down to the valley where they could play among the grasses and trees and bathe in the streams.

One hot day Canda anointed himself with sweet-smelling scent, made his meal of fruit pollen and dressed himself in flower gauze. Then, singing in sheer happiness, he began to

[1] The line over the last ā signifies the feminine gender.

amuse himself by swinging among the long creepers that grew near the stream.

After a while he left this play and went down to the stream with Candā to bathe and they sported in the water, splashing about and scattering the flowers that grew on its surface, enjoying themselves to their hearts' content. When they tired of this they came out of the water, put on their dresses of flowers and choosing a sandy spot where the sand was so fine and clean that it looked like silver, they spread a couch of flowers and lay down, full of happiness and contentment.

Soon Canda took a bamboo stick and began to play a tune and Candā danced, her soft hands moving to the rhythm of the music.

Into this idyllic scene came a human being.

A short time before this the king of Benares had decided to leave his kingdom for a while and go to the Himalayas. He had now reached the valley and stream where the fairies played, and hearing the sounds of the bamboo flute he moved towards it, taking care not to make any noise.

As soon as he saw Candā he fell in love with her and in order to possess her took up his bow and arrow and shot the fairy-husband. Canda cried out in pain and fell to the ground, turning himself away from his fairy-wife; but hearing him cry and seeing him turn away she hastened to him to find out what had happened. Finding that he had been wounded, she looked round for the cause and saw the king.

Rushing away from him, higher up the mountain, she turned and faced him, cursing him for what he had done.

You evil prince—ah woe is me ! my husband dear did wound,
Who there beneath a woodland tree now lies upon the ground.

O prince ! the woe that wrings my heart may thy own mother pay,
The woe that wrings my heart to see my fairy dead this day !

Yea, prince ! the woe that wrings my heart may thy own wife repay,
The woe that wrings my heart to see my fairy dead this day !

And may thy mother mourn her lord, and may she mourn her son
Who on my lord most innocent for lust this deed hast done.

And may thy wife look on and see the loss of lord and son,
For thou upon my harmless lord for lust this deed hath done.

When at last she paused the king answered her :

Weep not nor grieve: the woodland park has blinded you I ween:
A royal house shall honour thee, and thou shalt be my queen.

But Candā was the more infuriated at this insult and in a
voice as loud as a lion's roar called out:

What is this word thou hast said !
No ! I will surely slay myself ! Thine I will never be,
Who slew my husband innocent—all for lust of me.

Seeing that he could not possess her the king's passion died
as quickly as it had been aroused and saying: " I know that
creatures that feed on shrub and tree, love the woodland and
cannot be happy elsewhere," he turned away and went on his
journey.

As soon as he had gone Candā hurried back to her fairy-lord
and took his head on her lap, crying aloud in her pain:

Here in the hills and mountain caves, in many a glen and grot,
What shall I do, O fairy mine ! now that I see thee not ?

The wild beasts range, the leaves are spread on many a lovely spot
What shall I do, O fairy mine, now that I see thee not ?

As she sang she felt his hand and it was hot to her touch.

So, knowing now that he was not dead, she reproached the gods for not coming to her aid. Her devotion was so great that Sakka's [2] throne grew hot and he came down, disguised as a Brahmin, and offered to help. He sprinkled water on the wound and it healed up and soon Canda rose, well and strong as before. Delightedly the fairies thanked the Brahmin, and before he left he told them not to go down any more to the places where men moved, but to keep to the mountains.

Happy again, and carefree, the fairies moved away as Candā sang:

> To the mountains let us go
> Where the lovely rivers flow,
> Rivers all o'ergrown with flowers:
> There for ever, while the breeze
> Whispers in a thousand tones,
> Charm with talk the happy hours.

When the Master had finished he said: "Not now only, but long ago even as now, she was devoted and faithful of heart to me."

He identified the birth: Rahula's mother was Candā and "I myself was the fairy".

[2] Sakka, king of the gods, or Brahma.

THE WISHING TREE

ONCE, during the Buddha's earthly sojourn, there was a merchant who was friendly with a poor man and, though his friends tried to break the friendship, said that friendship did not depend on equality or inequality of external things. To show his trust he left his affairs in the hands of the poor friend when he went away and they prospered.

The Buddha told him:

> A friend rightly so-called is never inferior.
> The standard measure for friendship is ability to befriend,

and he told the following story.

Once the life that was to become the Buddha was born as the sprite that lived in a clump of kusa grass growing in the king's park. Near by was a Wishing Tree whose trunk was straight and tall and from which were many spreading branches. The king's own seat was near the tree for he was very fond of it. Between the sprite of the Wishing Tree and the sprite of the lowly kusa grass grew up a great friendship.

One day it was noticed that the pillar which supported the king's house was weak and another had to be found to replace it. The carpenters therefore searched for a tree trunk straight enough and tall enough and strong enough for the purpose. At last they came to the Wishing Tree and found what they needed. Knowing that the king was very fond of the tree they dare not cut it down before telling him, but when he heard that it was perfect for the new pillar he said, even though he was fond of it, it must be cut down.

12

The carpenters then took sacrifices to the tree and let it know that they were coming to cut it down on the next day.

When the Wishing Tree sprite heard this it burst into tears and its friends in the forest came to ask what was the matter. But though they were full of sympathy they could do nothing to help.

That night the Kusa Grass sprite called to see the Tree sprite and heard the news and determined to save his friend.

Changing himself into a chameleon, he went to the tree before the men came and got into the roots. Then he worked his way up to the branches, making the tree look full of holes. When he had finished he rested on a branch, his head moving from side to side.

In the morning the men came to saw the tree down but before beginning the leader struck the trunk with his hand. Of course it sounded as if it was rotten ! Turning away, he blamed them for not looking more carefully the day before, and they went to look for another tree.

All the Tree sprites sang the praises of the Kusa Grass sprite, for they said that they had not known how to help their friend even though they were stronger than the kusa grass. And the Wishing Tree sprite sang:

> Let great and small and equals, all,
> Do each their best, if harm befall,
> And help a friend in evil plight,
> As I was helped by Kusa sprite.

The Master identified the birth: Ananda was the Tree sprite and " I myself was the Kusa Grass sprite ".

THE MARSH CROW

ONE day the Brothers of the Order went on a visit to Devadatta and when they returned the Master asked Sariputta how Devadatta had greeted them.

Sariputta said he had imitated the Buddha.

Not for the first time, said the Buddha, had Devadatta imitated him and thereby come to grief, and he told them the following story.

Once the life that was to become the Buddha was born as a marsh crow. His name was Viraka and he lived near a pool from which he got his food.

About this time there was a famine in Kasa (Benares), and because of it people had no food left over to throw away to the crows, and to save themselves from starvation the crows left the city. One of them, Savitthaka, with his wife, went to the place where Viraka lived and made their home beside the pool.

Savitthaka watched how Viraka went down into the pool and ate fish and then came up and dried his feathers, so in order to have fish to eat he thought he would make friends with him by first becoming his servant. Accordingly he followed Viraka about until one day Viraka asked him what he wanted. Hearing that he wanted to serve him he agreed, and after that caught fish for himself and gave what was left to Savitthaka, who ate what he wanted and took the rest to his wife.

After a while pride rose in him: he thought that he looked like the crow, why could he not catch his own fish? He told Viraka of his desire, but Viraka warned him that he did not

14

belong to the same tribe as the marsh crows, and could not go into the water in the same way. In his pride Savitthaka did not listen to this advice but went into the pool, was caught in the weeds so that only the tip of his beak was above the water, could not breathe, and so died.

When he did not return his wife asked Viraka:

O have you seen Savitthaka, O Viraka, have you seen
My sweet-voiced mate whose neck is like the peacock in its sheen?

Viraka answered:

He was not born to dive beneath the wave,
    But what he could not do he needs must try;
So the poor bird has found a watery grave,
    Entangled in the weeds, and left to die.

The lady crow heard and wept, and returned to Kasa.

The Buddha identified the birth: Devadatta was Savitthaka, "I myself was Viraka."

THE GOLDEN PEACOCK

THE Master told this story when a backsliding Brother confessed that he had erred through his lust for pleasure. The Master explained to him that passion had before overthrown even holy beings who for seven thousand years had remained pure, and he told the following story.

Once the life that was to become the Buddha was born as a golden peacock. His mother laid her egg one day where she was eating and left it, and as with all healthy eggs—when not destroyed by a snake or otherwise interfered with—it cracked in time and a peachick came out. He was golden in colour, his eyes were like the gunja fruit, his beak red like coral, and three red streaks wound their way round his throat and passed down the middle of his back.

When he was full grown he was so beautiful and great that the peafowl made him their king.

One day as he was drinking from a pool he saw his reflection in the water and realized for himself that he was the most beautiful of peacocks. He thought further that if he stayed where men were he would fall into danger. So at nightfall, when the peafowl were away, he left the place and flew to the Himalayas, and passing over three ranges settled in a forest in the fourth where there was a great lake covered with lotuses. Nearby was a banyan tree and there he alighted. Near the tree was a hill, and in the heart of the hill was a pleasant cave. He flew down to it and alighted on a piece of flat land near its mouth. There he thought he would remain alone. None could climb to this place either from below or from above, and he was free from fear of man, wild animals or serpents.

Next morning he came out of the cave and sat on the hill-top facing the east. As the sun rose he protected himself for the coming day by reciting the verse, " There he rises, king all-seeing."

During the day he sought his food and in the evening he again sat on the top of a hill facing west, and as he watched the sun sinking he protected himself against the coming night by reciting the verse, " There he sets, the king all-seeing."

And so life passed.

One day a hunter living in the forest caught sight of him. When he was on the point of death he said to his son if ever the king wanted a golden peacock he would know where to find one.

One day the chief queen, just at early dawn, had a vision. She thought she saw a golden peacock preaching the Law and she listened, agreeing with all it said. The peacock finished and departed. She cried out in her sleep, " The king of the peacocks is escaping, catch him "—and she awoke.

She knew now it was a dream but she decided to ask the king to see if a golden peacock could be found. She would not tell him she had dreamt of one, for then he would not try to find it, but she told him she had a great desire to see one. As usual in such circumstances, the queen lay down and when the king visited her she told him she craved to hear the discourse of a golden peacock. If such a peacock could not be found, she said, she would die. The king promised to do what could be done and asked his courtiers where such a peacock could be found. They did not know and told him to ask the Brahmins. The Brahmins told him peacocks *could* be golden in colour, so hearing that it should be possible to find one he called his hunters together. None had seen a golden peacock, they said, but one said his father had told him of a place where one lived. The king gave him money and told him to find the peacock, catch him and bring him back.

The hunter went to the place and saw the peacock. But though he tried to snare him he failed and in due time died.

When the peacock could not be captured the queen also died and the king had the story written on a golden plate and placed in his treasury. The story said that the peacock was to be found in the fourth range of the Himalayas, and whoever ate his flesh would be for ever young and immortal. In due time the king himself died.

Another king read the story and sent out hunters. Other kings who followed him did the same, until six kings and six hunters had died.

Even the seventh hunter sent out by the seventh king could not catch it though he tried for seven years. Wondering why he was so difficult to snare he sat and watched him. Thus he saw that every morning and every evening the peacock watched the sun and recited his verse. He also noticed that there was no other peacock about, so this one must be a holy peacock and protected from harm by his holiness, and by his charm.

He therefore thought of a plan to beguile him and went to catch a peahen which he brought back with him. He taught her how to make her mating cry when he snapped his fingers at her, and how to dance when he clapped his hands, and then he set his snare as before. Then before the peacock had time to recite his verse, the man snapped his fingers and the peahen uttered her cry. The peacock heard and was so enamoured that he forgot his verse and went towards her and caught his feet in the snare.

Then the hunter saw what he had done—how he had betrayed the peacock who had been for so long safe from snares and full of virtue. He thought that to take him and give him to the king for the sake of a bribe would be unseemly and he thought he would set him free from the snare. But how? Such a big bird might break a wing or injure himself in other ways if he went near, for he would think the hunter came to kill him. So he went away for his bow and arrows, intending to break the snare.

Meanwhile the peacock wondered why he did not come and as he watched saw the hunter fitting his arrow. Thinking that he was about to be shot he said:

> If I being captured wealth to thee shall bring,
> Then wound me not, but take me still alive.
> I pray thee, friend, conduct me to the king:
> Methinks a most rich guerdon he will give.

The hunter replied:

> I have not set this arrow to the bow
> To do thee hurt, O peacock king, to-day:
> I wish to cut the snare and let thee go,
> Then follow thine own will and fly away.

Then they talked for some time of life and of right and wrong, and the hunter understood that it was wrong to kill or injure any living thing. He therefore renounced his hunter's craft.

He asked the peacock what he could do about the birds he had left in bondage at home, how could he set them free? The peacock told him to perform an Act of Truth, and then in all India there would no longer be any creature in bondage. This the hunter did:

> All those feathered fowl that I did bind,
> Hundreds and hundreds, in my house confined,
> Unto them all I give their life to-day,
> And freedom: let them homewards fly away.

Through this Act of Faith or Truth all the birds became free and went happily to their homes. All over India the same thing happened. No so much as a cat was confined !

And the peacock and the hunter rose to the skies.

Then the Master said the last verse:

> The hunter traversed all the forest land
> To catch the lord of peacocks, snare in hand.
> The glorious lord of peacocks he set free
> From pain, as soon as he was caught, like me.

After the great Truths had been given the backsliding Brother reached sainthood.

Then the Buddha identified the birth: " I was the peacock king."

THE FOREST FIRE

THIS story was told by the Buddha when he and his followers were on a journey near a jungle. Suddenly there was a great forest fire, and though the Master continued to walk towards it some of his followers were frightened and asked why they did not start a counter-fire. Others said that with the Buddha they would be safe.

The Master halted at a certain spot and his followers gathered round him. The fire still came on but presently it stopped and went out.

The Brothers praised the Buddha, but he told them it was not his present power that day which stopped the fire; it was through his power ages before, and he told them the following story.

Once the life that was to become the Buddha took form as a quail and lived with his father and mother in a nest in a forest.

As is usual in the bird-world the father and mother used to fly away every day to find food and bring it back to him, but though he fed on it he did not get strong and his wings were not powerful.

One night there was an uproar in the forest for all the animal and insect and bird life sensed a great forest fire creeping quickly to their part of the forest. All who could fled before it, including the parent quails. But the young quail was not strong enough to move and remained in the nest.

At first terror kept him motionless, but as the hissing of the fire got nearer, and the flames brighter, he became less afraid, and when the fire had come quite near he took his courage firmly in his hands. He said to himself that he could not fly or walk, he was without the protection of his parents and did not know what to do. As he thought he suddenly became aware of certain things, and said to himself that there was but a single principle in Nature. He would make an Act of Faith and force the flames to go back and so save himself and the rest of the birds. Then he spoke to the fire.

> With wings that fly not, feet that walk not yet,
> Forsaken by my parents, here I lie !
> Wherefore I conjure thee, dread Lord of Fire,
> Primaeval Jataveda,[1] turn ! go back !

The fire heard and stopped; then it went out suddenly, the smoke cleared, the animals and birds and insects came back again and the moon could once more be seen sailing serenely across the night sky. Once more peace and happiness reigned.

And the quail said:

> I wrought my Act of Truth, and therewithal
> The sheet of blazing fire left sixteen lengths
> Unscathed—like flames by water quenched.

This is one of the four wonders of the world, for through this Act of Truth made by the little quail, never will fire burn again in this part of the forest for all time.

The Buddha identified the birth: his present parents were the parents of the quail. " I myself was the quail."

[1] Jataveda, an old name of the god Fire.

THE LIONESS AND THE JACKAL

THIS story was told about an incident of the Buddha's day concerning a barber's son.

The barber who attended the palace was a Believer and attended to the Five Precepts [1] and the three Refuges [2].

One day he took his son with him to the palace and there the youth saw a well-born girl beautifully dressed and fell in love with her. When the youth got home he went to bed and grieved, saying that if he could not have the girl he would die. To have her, his father pointed out, was impossible, for she was high-born and he of low caste. He should not set his mind on forbidden fruit.

The youth, however, pined and died, and when the father had overcome his grief, he went to visit the Master, taking with him flowers, scent and perfumes.

The Master asked him why he had been so long away, and when he heard the reason he said that it was not the first time the youth had set his heart on something he could not have. And he told the following story.

Once the life that was to become the Buddha lived in a lion's body in a golden cave in the Himalayas which he shared with his parents, his six younger brothers and his sister. Every day the brothers went out to catch food, some of which they ate and some of which they brought back for their parents and sister.

[1] The *Pancha Sila* (see Introduction).
[2] I take Refuge in the Buddha.
I take Refuge in the Dhamma (the Law).
I take Refuge in the Sangha (the Brotherhood).

Higher up the mountain was a crystal cave in which a jackal lived where he could watch the lions. In time he fell in love with the lioness, but while her parents were alive he dared not approach her. When, however, the parents died and the brothers went out as usual to get food, he went down to her and told her of his love.

She was horrified at the insult, for lions are kings among beasts and jackals are very low in the animal kingdom, and she would have nothing to say to him. Sorrowfully he turned away and went to his cave where he lay down in despair.

The lioness wondered what she could do and decided that the only way to treat this insult was to refuse to eat and so die. But she thought she ought to tell her brothers first.

When the first brother arrived with food for her she told him what had happened, and he, looking up to the crystal cave, became so angry that he rushed up to destroy the jackal, thinking that it was lying in the sky. Of course he met the hard crystal walls and was killed, falling down to the bottom of the mountain.

The same thing happened to the other brothers in turn until the eldest arrived. He, too, looked up and saw the jackal, but he thought to himself that jackals do not lie in the sky. The animal must therefore be lying in a crystal cave. Wondering how he could destroy him he decided that there must be a way by which the jackal came down the mountain and he set out to find it. At the foot of the mountain he came across the dead bodies of his brothers and said to himself:

> Who rashly undertakes an enterprise,
> Not counting all the issue may arise,
>   Like one who burns his mouth in eating food
> Falls victim to the plans he did devise.

Then he climbed up the path and roared three times so loudly that the jackal, seeing him, burst his heart with fear and died.

The lion then returned to his sister, burying the dead bodies of his six brothers on the way.

The Master identified the birth: The barber's son was the jackal, the well-born girl the lioness, the six young lions the six Elders of the Buddha's Company, and " I myself was the eldest ".

THE LION AND THE JACKAL

THIS story was told about an incident happening in the Brotherhood.

One day Ananda was given five hundred cloths. He distributed them among five hundred Brothers. When the king who had given him the cloths asked him why he had done this he told him of the custom in the Order of having few things. The King then gave him five hundred more.

At that time Ananda was assisted by another Brother who did him many services and to him he gave this second five hundred cloths. The Brother then divided them among other members of the order.

But some Brothers complained to the Buddha, resenting the fact that Ananda had given all five hundred cloths to one Brother. The Buddha explained that one good turn deserves another and gratitude is a sound virtue. Ananda had chosen this way to show his gratitude to the serving Brother.

He then told the following story.

Once the life that was to become the Buddha took form as a lion and lived on a mountain. The mountain was surrounded by water, but near the foot an island of marshy grass-covered land rose just above the surface. Here many rabbits and deer lived.

One day the lion saw a deer grazing there and jumped towards her. She fled in terror. But the lion could not stop himself in his flight and fell into the wet muddy ground. The mud was so thick that it held his four feet fast, and he stayed caught for seven days without food.

On the seventh day a jackal saw him and ran away terrified. The lion, sensing a possible rescuer, called after him and asked him to come back and help to release him from the mud. Very slowly the jackal approached and seeing that the lion was really caught began to push the mud away from his feet, making a channel down which the water could come and make the mud softer. Then he got beneath the lion's body and asked him to make one great effort to free himself while he pushed from underneath.

This idea worked well and the lion was freed.

Once on dry land the lion's great need was food and seeing a bull he killed it. Full of gratitude to the jackal he offered him his share of the meat first, and then ate some himself. When both of them had satisfied their hunger the jackal took some more food. Surprised at this the lion asked him why, when he was satisfied, he took more, and the jackal told him he was taking some for his wife. Taking some for his own wife also the lion and the jackal started for home. First they went to the jackal's home and fed the she-jackal. Then the lion took them both with him to his cave and told them if they would live in the small cave at the entrance to his cave he would look after them.

This was agreed upon and the two families lived happily together for some time, the young lions playing with the young jackals, and all felt safe under the lion's protection.

After a time, however, the peaceful state was disrupted. The lioness began to wonder why her husband was so attentive to the jackals and she began to feel jealous. She told her children of this and they began to throw out hints to the young jackals that all was not well, and she herself hinted to the she-jackal that it was time the family removed themselves.

Soon the she-jackal told her husband, and one day when the

lion and the jackal were out together, the jackal asked the lion why he had not asked him to leave if he wanted him to go away ? Naturally, the jackal said, he would go at once.

The strong will always have their way; it is their nature so to do; Your mate roars loud; and now I say I fear what once I trusted to.

The lion was amazed and said he did not want him to leave at all and asked why he had thought he did.   So the story came out.   Going home, the lion reminded his wife of the time when for seven days he had been caught in the mud, and he told her of the jackal's help and of the reason for his friendship with him.   The lioness now understood and the two families lived again together in friendship.

A friend who plays a friendly part, however small and weak he be, He is my kinsman and my flesh and blood, a friend and comrade he; Despise him not, my sharp-fanged mate ! this Jackal saved my life for me.

The Buddha identified the birth: Ananda was the jackal, " I myself was the lion."

JACKAL BEWARE!

ONCE some of the Brethren visited Devadatta and on their return the Buddha asked them how they had been received.

Sariputta said that Devadatta had imitated the Buddha and had got himself into trouble thereby.

Then the Master said, not for the first time had Devadatta got himself into trouble by this means, and he told the following story.

Once the life that was to become the Buddha dwelt as a lion in a cave in the Himalayas. One day after killing a buffalo and eating all he wanted he drank water and made his way to his cave. A jackal saw him coming and being frightened and seeing no way of escape lay down in his path. In answer to the lion's question why he was doing such a thing the jackal said he wished to serve him. That being so the lion agreed and took him home to his cave, and after this gave him what food he did not need himself. The jackal therefore got quite fat, and proud.

One day he told the lion that he was giving him much trouble in always finding food for him and he would himself go out and kill an elephant and after eating his fill would bring some back to him.

The lion told him that he did not belong to the breed of animal that could kill an elephant and eat it: he would him-self go out and kill one and bring back some meat for him. And he begged him not to take on more than he could possibly do.

Jackal beware !
   His tusks are long.
     One of thy puny race
 Would scarcely dare
   So huge and strong
     A beast as this to face.

But the jackal would not listen and leaving the cave roared the jackal's cry three times.

Down in the valley he saw an elephant and thinking to land on its head he jumped down. But turning a somersault in the air the poor jackal fell at the feet of the elephant instead, and was crushed beneath the elephant's foot and lay groaning till he died.

The lion looked down and saw the jackal lying there and said:

   A jackal once assumed a lion's pride,
   And elephant as equal foe defied.
   Prone on the earth, while groans his bosom rent,
   He learned the rash encounter to repent.

   Who thus should challenge one of peerless fame,
   Nor mark the vigour of his well-knit frame,
   Shares the sad fate that on the jackal came.

   But who the measure of his own power knows,
   And nice discretion in his language shows,
   True to his duty lives and triumphs o'er his foes.

In this way did the Buddha show what are the proper duties to do in the world.

The Master identified the birth: Devadatta was the jackal, "I myself was the lion."

THE LION-JACKAL

THERE was a member of the Order, Kokalika, who hearing some of the Brethren preach, wanted to do likewise. But he only showed up his own inferiority.

But Buddha, on hearing this, said it was not the first time that his voice had betrayed his true worth, and he told the following story.

Once a lion and a jackal mated and a cub was born. Its toes, claws, mane, colour and figure were that of a lion, but his voice was that of a jackal.

One day after the rains all the lion cubs were playing together and roared out in fun. The lion-jackal roared too, but his voice made the jackal sound and all the other cubs became silent.

Another son of the lion went to his father and asked why that cub looked like a lion and roared like a jackal:

> Lion's claws and lion's paws,
> Lion's feet to stand upon;
> But the bellow of this fellow
> Sounds not like a lion's son !

The father told his son the reason for this and then sent for the lion-jackal cub. He advised him never to roar because:

> All will see what kind you be
> If you yelp as once before;
> So don't try it, but keep quiet;
> Your's is not a lion's roar.

The Master identified the birth. Kokalika was the lion-jackal, Rahula the brother cub, "The king of beasts was I myself."

31

THE LION AND THE BOAR

ONE night after the Buddha had spoken to the Brothers and a crowd of bystanders he retired to his cell. When he had gone one of the Brothers asked Sariputta many questions, all of which he answered, and all listened entranced to his wisdom. That is, all but one. This Elder thought to himself that if he could ask a question which Sariputta could not answer all men would think how clever he was, and he asked a stupid question.

Sariputta looked at him, realized that he knew nothing, and without saying a word rose and retired to his cell.

The bystanders were furious at this for they said the Elder had prevented them from listening to wisdom and they called out, " Seize this wicked man."

The Elder fled, and not seeing it in time fell into a hole in the cover of a cesspool just outside the monastery and was, of course, covered with filth.

Then people felt sorry for him and went to tell the Master what had happened. When he heard them he said this was not the first time the Elder had come to grief by being puffed up with pride, and he told the following story.

Once when the life that was to become the Buddha took form as a lion and lived in a cave in the Himalayas a boar lived near him, one of a number of boars dwelling near a lake.

One day after the lion had killed and eaten he went to the lake to drink and saw a boar feeding at the lakeside. Deciding that he would kill the boar another day the lion hid so that the boar would not be frightened and not come again. But the boar did see him, and being proud, thought the lion was frightened of him ! He therefore challenged him to fight.

The lion refused but said that in a week they could fight.

The boar was delighted and told all the other boars, for he was proud to think that a lion had been frightened of him and he felt sure he could kill him. But the boars let him know that he could never be a match for a lion and they advised him to take measures to safeguard himself. He was advised to roll in all the filth he could find every day for six days, letting it dry on him. On the seventh day he was to let it get wet. It would then smell horribly, and when the lion came he should take care to get between the wind and the lion so that the smell would reach the lion.

This he did. But the smell was so horrid that the lion refused to fight him, for he would not even touch such filth with his foot. He said:

O dirty Boar, your hide is foul, the stench is horrible to me;
If you would fight I yield me quite, and own you have the victory.

The Boar was now prouder than ever, but the other boars left the place, feeling sure the lion would return one day and kill them.

The Master identified the birth: The Boar was the Elder and " I myself was the lion ".

THE END OF THE WORLD

ONE day the disciples saw some false ascetics lying on thorns, torturing themselves by fire, etc., and they asked the Buddha if there was any special merit in these kinds of penance. He told them that there was no merit in them, for they had been examined and tested and they proved to be like the noise heard by the hare.

He then told them the following story.

Once the life that was to become the Buddha was born as a lion, and lived in a wood near the western ocean. Nearby was a grove of palm trees mixed with vilva trees and beneath a palm sapling at the foot of a vilva tree lived a hare.

One day the hare lay beneath the young tree and thought to himself—if the earth should be destroyed, what would become of me?

At that very moment a ripe vilva fruit fell on a palm leaf with a loud plop. The hare heard the noise and thought, this is indeed the end of the earth, for it is collapsing, and he fled without looking behind.

Another hare saw him running and asked the cause. "Pray don't ask me," he said. The other hare ran with him and asked again, "What is it?" The first hare stopped and without looking behind said the earth was breaking up, and then ran on again. Soon more hares joined them and in time a hundred thousand hares were running. Other animals saw them, a deer, a boar, an elk, a buffalo, a wild ox, a rhinoceros, a tiger, a lion, an elephant, and so on, and all asked in turn why they were running away. The same answer was given.

When our lion heard the reason for this mad flight, he thought to himself, the earth is not coming to an end; the hare must have misunderstood some sound. He realized, too, that if he did not do something all the animals would perish for they were rushing to disaster. Getting ahead of them, he stopped at the foot of a mountain and roared three times.

The animals paused, huddled together in fear, while the lion went among them and asked why they were running away. When he heard that the earth was collapsing he asked the elephant if he had seen it doing so. The elephant said he had not, but the lion had. The lion said he had not, but the tiger had, the tiger said the rhinoceros had, the rhinoceros said the wild ox, and so on until at last the hare was reached. The lion asked the hare if this was true, and he said it was, for he had seen it. Where had it been seen, asked the lion. Near the ocean, answered the hare. Then the lion thought that a ripe fruit must have fallen and made a noise and the hare had been frightened into a rash conclusion.

He now reasoned with the animals and said he would go with the hare and find out if it was true. At first the hare was frightened, but at last got on the lion's back and went with him to find the place. When they had nearly reached it the hare was too frightened to go on and said:

> From the spot where I did dwell
>   Issued forth a fearful " thud ";
> What it was I could not tell,
>   Nor what caused it understood.

So the lion went alone to the foot of the tree and there he found the ripe vilva fruit. But the earth had not cracked ! He made the hare look too, and then they went back to the other animals, and told them. The Buddha said:

Alarmed at sound of fallen fruit
   A hare once ran away,
The other beasts all followed suit
   Moved by that hare's dismay.

They hastened not to view the scene
   But lent a willing ear
To idle gossip, and were clean
   Distraught with foolish fear.

They who to Wisdom's calm delight
   And Virtue's heights attain,
Though ill example should invite,
   Such passing fear disdain.

The Master identified the birth saying, "I was the lion."

THE HARE

ONCE the Buddha and his Brotherhood were welcomed and fed by a landowner for many days. At the end the Buddha told this old legend to show that it was a tradition of the wise men to sacrifice even themselves to beggars.

Once the life that was to become the Buddha took form as a hare and made his home in a forest near a stream of fresh water, so clean and clear that it looked as blue as lapis lazuli. The grass nearby was green and tender and soft to the touch of the feet of the animals who lived there. The trees were full of flowers and fruit. It was such a verdant spot, and the jungle round it was so pleasant with creeping plants and trees that men had also begun to live there.

The hare, though strong, was gentle. He was also wise, and in time the other animals who lived in this part of the forest began to look up to him as though he were their king. Three of them became his special friends—a monkey, a jackal, and an otter—and every evening they sat together and talked of many things. Gradually their character began to change and many bad habits were dropped, including the habit of stealing, and they became friendly towards all the other animals.

One evening as they sat together, and the moon, nearly at the full, was shining very brightly in the dark midnight sky, the hare told his friends that by its appearance he could tell that the following day would be a holy day. He told them it was, therefore, a good thing if they all arranged not to eat anything that day but to give whatever food they found to anyone who asked for it. Quite cheerfully they agreed to do so.

In the morning the monkey went to the mountain nearby and gathering some ripe mango fruits took them back to his home. There he put them aside and sat waiting to see if any-one would come for them. And he thought to himself that if no one came he would have a good meal the next day.

The jackal found a lizard and a pot of milk-curds outside a hut, and asking aloud if they belonged to anyone and not re-ceiving any answer, took the cord attached to the pot of curds and placed it round his neck, picked up the lizard and went home. Then, like the monkey, he sat and wondered if anyone would ask for them. He thought, too, that if no one wanted them he would have a good meal the next day.

The otter found some fish in the sand by the river where they had been placed by a fisherman. He asked aloud if they be-longed to anyone, and receiving no reply took them home. Then he sat and waited, and thought of the good meal he would have the next day if no one wanted them.

The hare started out to get his food, which was grass. Sud-denly he realized that men did not eat grass and therefore he had nothing to offer. After worrying for a little while he remembered that men ate flesh. All the flesh he had to offer was his own body and he decided, with joy in his heart, that he would offer his body to anyone who asked for food.

The force of this great vow was felt by the whole earth. The mountains shook with joy, the oceans stirred to their depths, the air seemed full of music and the sky full of glorious colours. Lightning flashed and thunder rolled gently, making a very pleasing sound. Flowers fell around him and the wind in tribute blew their pollen over him.

Sakka, lord of the Devas, heard the vow and thought he would put it to the test. So, at noon, he went to the forest making himself look like a poor lonely traveller, and cried out that he had lost his caravan and was hungry and tired. He begged for help.

When he came near the monkey he called again for help. The monkey immediately offered him the mango fruit but he refused it saying if he needed it he would come again later on. Hearing his cry the otter offered his fish but it was also refused. The jackal offered the lizard and the pot of curds but they, too, were refused, the traveller saying he would come again if he needed them.

When he came to the hare the hare immediately offered his own body as food. Then a problem arose: how could a man kill someone who had been kind to him? Such a thing was not possible.

In consternation the hare pondered.

While he thought, Sakka caused a charcoal fire to appear behind him, with golden flames and without smoke. As soon as the hare saw it he rushed towards it and shaking his body three times and calling to any little insect that might be in his fur to come out, he jumped into the middle of the flames joyfully as a bird drops into a bed of lotuses.

The flames did not feel hot to him, but cool and refreshing, and Sakka, with his jewelled hands, soft and white like the petals of the lotus, lifted him up and took him to heaven. There he told the heavenly beings of this wonderful sacrifice, and to commemorate it for all time he caused an image of the hare to appear on his palace, Vaigravanta, and another on Sudharma, the Hall of the Devas. And with the juice he obtained from a mountain, he drew, for all men to see, the figure of the hare on the face of the moon. There it will remain until the end of the great period of time in which we live, as a reminder of the sacrifice of the hare.

This is one of the great marvels of our age.

The Buddha identified the birth: Moggallana was the jackal, Ananda the otter, Sariputta the monkey. "I myself was the hare."

O GOLDEN FOOT

THIS story was told about a girl member of the Sisterhood who, well-born, was married to an unbeliever. She was, however, allowed to do as she pleased and one day invited her husband to listen to the Buddha. He then became a believer.

Once the life that was to become the Buddha took form as a stag. He grew up beautiful and graceful, of golden colour, with his feet firm and glossy as lacquer, his horns curved like a silver wreath, his eyes like round jewels and his mouth like a ball of crimson wool. With his wife, a lovely doe, he lived happily and he had a large following of dappled deer.

Unfortunately one day his foot was caught in a snare set by a hunter, and though he tugged and tugged he could not free himself and he called out the cry of capture. The herd fled. When the doe saw that he was not with them she returned and seeing him fast begged him to try and break away.

> O Golden-Foot, no effort spare
> To loose thyself from thongèd snare.
> How could I joy, bereft of thee,
> To range amidst the woodland free?

The stag replied:

> I spare no effort, but in vain,
> My liberty I cannot gain.
> The more I struggle to get loose,
> The sharper bites the thongèd noose.

Hearing this, the doe said she would save him.

Soon she saw the hunter approaching and went to meet him, singing the praises of her husband, king of the herd, asking him:

> Let on the earth a leafy bed,
> Hunter, where we may fall, be spread;
> And drawing from its sheath thy sword,
> Slay me and afterwards my lord.

The hunter was so amazed that he set the stag free, and in her fullness of happiness the doe said:

> As I to-day rejoice to see
> This mighty beast at liberty,
> So, hunter, that didst loose the gin,
> Rejoice with all thy kith and kin.

In return for what he had done the stag gave him a magic jewel and told him to use it to set up a household, to give alms and show goodwill to all, for that was his Path; not for him to become an ascetic.

He identified the birth: Channa was the hunter; the female novice the doe, " I myself was the stag."

THE ANTELOPE

WHEN the Brethren were discussing Devadatta's attempts to kill the Buddha by hurling rocks, hiring archers and setting the elephant on him, the Buddha asked them what they were discussing. When he heard he told them the following story to show that Devadatta had tried before to kill him, and failed.

Once the life that was to become the Buddha was born as an antelope and lived in a forest, eating fruit.

One day a deerstalker saw his footmarks near a tree and built a platform in the tree so that he could sit there and catch him when he came again for fruit.

The antelope came as usual on the next day but the thought struck him that sometimes men hid to kill deer and he had better wait and watch for a bit before he went nearer the tree.

After a time the deerstalker became impatient and taking some of the fruit threw it towards the antelope, hoping to attract him nearer. But he forgot that fruit which falls from a tree falls down straight, and not outward from the tree, and the antelope, seeing the fruit come towards him, asked the tree if it had changed its normal habit! He thought he had better not venture nearer (he said) and he told the tree that he would eat from another tree that day!

The deerstalker called after him that he had saved himself that day—"I have missed you this time"—but on another day he would catch him.

The Buddha answered: " Yes, but you have not missed the reward of your conduct ! "

The Master identified the birth: Devadatta was the hunter. " I myself was the antelope."

THE ANTELOPE, THE TORTOISE AND THE WOODPECKER

THIS story was told by the Buddha when the news was brought to him one day that Devadatta was plotting to kill him. "Ah, Brethren," he said, "it was just the same long ago; Devadatta tried then to kill me, as he is trying now." And he told the following story.

Once the life that was to become the Buddha took birth as an antelope and lived in a thicket near a lake. Not far from him lived a woodpecker whose nest was on the top of a tree. In the lake lived a tortoise. These three became firm friends.

One day a hunter saw the footmarks of the antelope and set a trap to catch him.

In the evening the antelope went as usual to the lake to drink, but his foot got caught fast in the trap. His cries of terror and pain were heard by the woodpecker and the tortoise and both rushed to his aid. When they saw what had happened they knew that the hunter would return, so a plan was formed to rescue their friend. The woodpecker said:

Come, Tortoise, tear the leathern snare and bite it through
   and through,
And of the hunter I'll take care, and keep him off from you.

So, while the tortoise with its sharp teeth tried to cut the leather the woodpecker flew away to the house of the hunter and waited there.

In the very early morning the hunter took his knife and started to leave his house by the front door. But the woodpecker was waiting and flew at him, flapping his wings in his face. The man went back into his house, saying to himself that the omens were against him.

Later on he tried to leave by the back door, but the same thing happened and the woodpecker's wings struck his face again. So he re-entered his house and decided to wait till morning came and the omens were better.

The woodpecker then flew back to his friends. He found the tortoise, his mouth bleeding from his efforts, still trying to free the antelope, for one last strand remained uncut. But just then they saw the hunter approaching. The woodpecker flew away to the top of his tree, the antelope, seeming to get extra strength from his fear, made a great effort and the strand broke, and he fled into the forest. Only the tortoise remained, for he was too weak to move.

The hunter saw the tortoise and picking him up put him in his bag and hung the bag on a tree. Then he saw the antelope who had been watching what had happened to his friend. The antelope let the man see him and then, making pretend that he was very weak, went deep into the forest, followed by the hunter. After going for some way he slipped back, took the bag down from the tree with his horns and freed the tortoise. The woodpecker now flew down from his tree and the friends were together once more.

But the antelope knew the hunter would return and told the woodpecker he should find another home and they would all separate. So:

The tortoise went into the pool, the deer into the wood,
And from the tree the woodpecker carried away his brood.

Finally the hunter returned and found that he had lost antelope, tortoise and bag, and sad and weary he returned to his home.

But the three friends continued to live happily in their separate homes.

The Buddha identified the birth: Devadatta the huntsman, Sariputta the woodpecker, Moggallana the tortoise, and " I was the antelope ".

ROHANTA THE GOLDEN STAG

ONE day the Brethren discussed Ananda and his willingness to lay down his life for the Master. When the Buddha asked them what they were discussing, and they told him, he said that not for the first time had Ananda given his life for him, and he told the following story.

Once the life that was to become the Buddha was born as a golden-coloured stag and was called Rohanta. When he grew up he was the leader of eighty thousand deer. He lived with his brother Chitta-migra and his sister Sutana, and looked after his old and blind parents.

About this time a Queen had a dream. She dreamt that she saw a golden stag sitting on a golden throne teaching the people, but before the talk was finished she awoke, and thinking that it was real, shouted to her attendants to " catch that stag ". Naturally as they knew there was no stag, they laughed !

But the dream had made such an impression on her that she determined to see and hear the stag, for it must, she felt, exist somewhere. Accordingly hunters were sent out to find it.

This news reached the son of the hunter who had seen Rohanta and he went to the place and set a snare to catch him.

The following night Rohanta and the herd went down to the lake as usual to drink and his foot was caught in the snare. When he found that he could not move he did not cry out the cry of capture lest the herd should take fright and run away

48

before they had drunk their fill. But as soon as they had finished and were ready to leave he tried to pull himself free. Three times he tried, but though the thong cut through his flesh to the bone he was held fast. Then, and only then, did he cry the cry of capture and, hearing this, the herd, including his brother and sister, fled.

After running for some way Chitta-migra looked for his brother, and when he could not find him turned back to see if it was he who had been caught. When Rohanta saw him he begged him to go away, for if he was caught too who would look after their parents? But Chitta-migra said:

> No, no, Rohanta, I'll not go: my heart has drawn me near;
> I'm ready to lay down my life, I will not leave thee here.

While they were talking Sutana came and joined them, for when she too had looked for her brother and had not found him she had returned. Once again Rohanta begged her to leave him if for no other reason than the care of their parents. But she would not:

> I'll lose my life but never leave thee snared and captured here.

It was thus that the hunter found them when he came with his spear ready to kill. Poor Sutana was terrified when she saw him and ran away—but she came back. As the hunter afterwards told the king:

> The tender doe in passing fear a little way did fly,
> Then did a thing most hard to do, for she returned to die.

When the hunter saw the devotion and courage of the three he could not bring himself to kill. Instead he cut the snare and laid the stag by the water's edge, loosened the noose and

washed away the blood. Full of sorrow he bathed the wound
and rubbed the tender leg so that it healed quickly and became
as it had been before.

Then Chitta-migra said to him:

Hunter, be happy now, and may thy kindred happy be.
As I am happy to behold the mighty stag set free.

Rohanta asked the hunter why he had snared him. Was it
on his own behalf or on some other? And when the hunter
told him of the king's wish and the queen's dream, he asked
to be taken to the king. This the hunter refused to do, for he
said the king might hurt him. So Rohanta told him to brush
his back with his hand. The hunter did so and found the hand
full of beautiful golden hairs. Asking what he should do with
them, Rohanta told him to take them to the king and queen,
tell them about him and preach to them ten stanzas of a poem
which he would teach him.

When the hunter was proficient he started on his journey
accompanied for some way by the three deer who afterwards
returned home to their parents.

The hunter did as he was bidden, and showed the hairs to the
king and repeated his discourse to the king and queen. The
king gave him many presents in return but he gave them to his
wife and for himself, asked permission to become an ascetic,
for:

Into my hands the creature came, into my privy snare,
And was fast caught: but others, free, attended on him there.

Then pity made my flesh to creep, a pity strange and new,
If I should slay this deer (thought I) then I shall perish too.

Before leaving he begged the king to do righteously to friends and courtiers, in war and travel, in town and village, to Brahmins and ascetics, to beasts and birds, and

> With watchful vigilance on the path of goodness go.

The Buddha identified the birth: Channa was the huntsman, Sariputta the king, a sister of the Order was the queen, Uppalavanna was Sutana, Ananda was Chitta, the Sakya clan the eighty thousand deer, and "I myself was the stag".

THE STAG AND THE KING

ONCE a Brother performed a miracle in public and the Buddha rebuked him for using his powers in an unworthy way, and he forbade the use of any miraculous powers the Brethren possessed.

The Brother had made himself rise in the air so that he could take down a bowl which had been placed on a high pole as a test by the unbelievers as to the miraculous powers of the Brothers. But the unbelievers said that they could easily perform miracles themselves and if the Buddha performed one they would make one twice as good.

When the Brothers told this to the Buddha he said if they performed a miracle he would perform one.

The king of the time asked him how he could perform a miracle when such performances were banned? But the Buddha asked him if he would refrain from picking a fruit in his garden because he had ordered that men should not pick the fruit? The command not to perform miracles rested on the Brothers, not on the Buddha himself, and he let it be known that he would perform a miracle on the full moon of June. Proclamation was made to this effect and crowds gathered.

On the morning after the full moon the Buddha went out as usual with his begging bowl and when he was at the palace gate the gardener saw him, and gave him a beautiful ripe mango which he had picked for the king. The Buddha took it and sat down to eat it. When he had finished he gave the stone to Ananda and asked him to give it to the gardener, asking him to bury it at that spot. This, he said, would be the miracle.

Immediately the stone was planted, it burst, roots and leaves appeared and it grew into a very tall tree. Blossoms came,

52

then the fruit, swarms of bees buzzed round, the wind came and blew the ripe fruit off and the Brothers ate it.

Then he performed another marvellous miracle.

One day later he saw that people admired the Brothers who could perform miracles whereas Sariputta's wisdom not being so apparent was not recognized. He therefore asked the Brothers many questions, and then one which only Sariputta could answer, and the people perceived his wisdom.

When the Brothers discussed this and the Buddha heard of their discussion he said he would tell them a story.

Once the life that was to become the Buddha took birth as a stag.

Now the king of that part of the country decided one day to go on a hunting expedition and calling his courtiers together told them that whoever let a deer go by that day should be punished. The men then made a pact among themselves to drive whatever deer there were straight to the king, and in this way a stag was driven towards him. The king shot his arrow but missed, for stags have a way of escaping arrows sometimes, and this stag rolled over so that the arrow did not meet his flesh. The king saw him fall and thought he had killed him and sang out in his triumph. But the courtiers laughed, for the stag got up and ran away !

The king was naturally angry at their laughter and determined to get the stag and followed it as quickly as he could. As they ran they passed near a pit overgrown with weeds, the bottom filled with water and the stag, smelling the water, turned aside, but the king could not stop himself and fell into it.

As the stag ran on he realized that the king was no longer running after him for the footsteps had stopped, and he thought to himself that he must have fallen into a pit. So he turned back and, looking over the edge, saw the king at the bottom. He told him not to fear for he would save him, and supporting himself on a rock he drew him up. Then he put the king on his back and running back set him down not far from the courtiers. Before leaving him he admonished him for his treatment of animals. The grateful king asked him to come to Benares with him, but he would not.

The following morning the king awoke early and chanted aloud some verses in connection with this event without giving the details. His chaplain heard him and realiz ng what had happened, said to the king:

> The stag that on a mountain steep thy quarry was of late,
> He bravely gave thee life, for he was free from greed and hate.
>
> Out of the horrid pit, out of death's jaws,
>   Leaning upon a rock (a friend at need)
> The great stag saved thee: so thou saidst with cause,
>   His mind is far aloof from hate or greed.

Now the king was very fond of shooting, and, though he no longer killed animals, often practised with a target. One day while thus practising with his chaplain by his side he poised his arrow ready to shoot when between him and the target appeared the stag. Sakka, King of the gods, had caused it to appear to be there to test the king, and taking over the body of the chaplain he told the king to shoot. The king refused, even though threatened with death, even though his wife and family should be killed, for, he said:

> Once in a grisly forest full of dread,
>   That very stag saved me from hopeless woe.
> How can I wish my benefactor dead
>   After such service done me long ago !

Sakka was pleased and appeared in his own form saying:

> Live long on earth, O true and faithful friend !
>   Comfort with truth and goodness this domain;
> Then hosts of maidens round thee shall attend
>   While thou as Indra [1] mid the gods shalt reign.
>
> From passion free, with ever-peaceful heart,
>   When strangers crave, supply their weary need;
> As power is given thee, give, and play thy part,
>   Blameless, till heaven shall be thy final meed.

The Buddha identified the birth saying that at this time also Sariputta knew the details of the story although only the general terms had been given, for Sariputta was the chaplain, Ananda the king, and " I myself was the stag ".

[1] King of the heaven-world.

BANYAN THE GOLDEN DEER

THE story was told by the Buddha about the mother of an Elder among his Brotherhood.

As a young girl, daughter of a rich merchant, she had asked to be allowed to take up the religious life but her parents refused to let her. She thought that when she had married perhaps she would be allowed to follow her wish, and in due time she married and lived a good and virtuous life.

One day, a festival day, when everyone was attired in their richest clothes, she did not adorn herself and her husband asked her why. She told him that the body was full of disease and would die in time; why should she anoint it and adorn it with fine clothes? For some time they discussed these questions and at last the husband realized that her desire was to become a Sister and he agreed that she should do so, and took her himself to the following of Devadatta.

She was very happy for a time, but one day discovered that she was going to have a child. Her fellow Sisters saw this too, and took her to Devadatta asking what ought to be done.

Devadatta thought to himself that it would look bad for his followers if one of his Sisterhood bore a child, and it would seem that he condoned it. Therefore without finding out anything further as to when the child was conceived, before or after her entering the Order, he expelled her.

The Sister told her fellows that Devadatta was not the Buddha and she would go and ask him to take her.

When she approached him he thought that the unbelievers would say that the Buddha took those whom Devadatta had expelled, and in order that all should know the truth he called together all his followers. Then he asked to be informed as to when the child was conceived. When it was found out that this was before the woman had entered the Sisterhood she was told she could return to the nunnery.

In due time the child was born. The king of the city heard it cry one day and said that a nunnery was not the right place to bring up a child so took him to his palace where in time he grew into a good and holy man. He was now one of the greatest of the Buddha's following.

One day the Brethren were talking of this and how Devadatta had nearly prevented the birth of such a wise man, and how the Buddha's love had proved their salvation. Just then the Buddha came and asked what they were talking about. When they told him, he said that was not the first time such a thing had happened, and he told them the following story.

Once the life that was to become the Buddha took form as a golden deer, as tall as a young foal. His body was perfect: his horns gleamed like polished silver, his eyes were like two jewels, his mouth a clear bright red, his hoofs hard and firm like lacquer, and his tail was as long as a yak's. His name was Banyan and he ruled over five hundred deer who lived in a forest near Benares.

There was another herd of five hundred deer in the same forest and it was ruled over by another golden deer whose name was Branch.

Life ought to have been happy for them but it was not. Day by day the king hunted in the forest, and, in order to make the hunt successful, citizens, both shop-keepers and field-workers, were ordered to leave their work and round up the deer. This meant that their own work or business was neglected and they became discontented.

One day they thought of a plan. Near the king's palace was the royal park, and the men decided to dig lakes and sow grass on it, and then drive the deer there from the forest. Then the king could hunt in the park and they would not be needed to round up the deer. When they had finished their work they told the king what they had done, and why, and henceforth the king hunted there daily.

Only one deer each day was needed for the royal table but it is difficult to be sure that each arrow would kill and not merely wound. So though one deer was killed each day many more were injured. This was very upsetting for the herd and worrying for the two leaders.

One day Banyan thought of a plan. Why should not one deer voluntarily go to the killing-block at the palace every day, one day from his herd and one day from Branch's herd. Thus the rest would be safe from harm. All agreed to this. Only Banyan and Branch were exempted for the king had one day seen them and had ordered that they were never to be killed.

For a time all went well, but one day a young doe, herself with young, found it was her turn to go. She went to her leader, Branch, and asked if she might take her turn when the little one was born and able to be left, but Branch was adamant and said that no change could be made. She must take her turn.

The sorrowful young mother-to-be went then to Banyan. He at once said kindly to her that she must not worry ; he would arrange that another took her place, and gladly she went away.

Banyan then went himself to the killing-block and laid down his head for slaughter. But when the man whose duty it was to kill the deer saw that it was the golden stag which had presented itself he dared not kill. The king was told and went himself to see why this had happened. Speaking kindly to Banyan, the king asked why he had come when he knew that his life had been spared.

When he heard of the young doe the king's heart was touched and he granted her life when her turn came to die. But Banyan asked him if he could also think of the herds and spare their lives. The king consented. Banyan, still unsatisfied, asked what about all other animals, birds and fish in the kingdom? All lived in fear of death! The king said he would spare their lives also, for love had come into his heart and no one killed that which they loved.

Satisfied at last, Banyan returned to the herd and all lived in peace. In due time the doe gave birth to a son and when he grew up she told him to follow Banyan in all he did.

In this new-found freedom the deer were happy, but they began to leave the park and eat the crops in the fields outside and the people complained to the king. He told them he could not go back on his word for promises were sacred.

Fortunately Banyan heard of this and calling his herd together he told them it was not right to eat the crops. Then he told the peasants not to fence in their lands but to put up a tablet or sign near them, and then the deer would not go into those fields.

This was done and henceforth friendship and peace reigned in the kingdom between man and beast for many years.

The Master identified the birth: Ananda was the king, the present Sister was the doe, her deer-son was the son of today, Devadatta was Branch and " I myself was Banyan ".

THE CROCODILE AND THE MONKEY

THIS story was told by the Buddha when he heard of yet another murderous attempt by Devadatta to destroy him. This was not the first time he had made attempts to kill him (he said) and told the following story.

Once the life that was to become the Buddha took form as a monkey and lived on the banks of a wide river in the middle of which was an island where mangoes and other fruit grew in great abundance.

Every day he went to the island for his food, returning home in the evening. To reach it he took two great leaps, one that took him to a rock about halfway to the island, and the other that brought him to the foot of the fruit trees.

Unfortunately a crocodile lived in the river with his wife, and often saw the monkey make these journeys. The crocodile-wife thought that such a large and beautiful monkey would be good to eat and she asked her husband to catch him for her one day as he returned home.

That day when the monkey was ready to return he looked across at the rock. It seemed further out of the water than usual, yet this could not be so because the water had not fallen. He reasoned with himself that the only explanation for the phenomenon was that something was sitting on the rock—perhaps a crocodile. He thought, therefore, that he had better make sure that all was well before he took his usual leap, and he called out to the rock three times. Naturally he got no response and to make quite sure he asked the rock why he was not talking to him that day !

The crocodile thought to himself that if the rock usually answered the monkey he ought to do so himself and so he asked him what he wanted.

The monkey replied: " Who are you ? "

" I am a crocodile," said the crocodile. And, he added, he was going to catch and eat him.

There was no other way home for the monkey so what could he do ? After a time he thought of the answer. He called to the crocodile and asked him to open his mouth so that he could catch him as he jumped. The crocodile did so, and the monkey jumped on to his head and leapt from there to the other bank quite safely, because crocodiles always close their eyes when they open their mouths.[1] When the crocodile saw what had taken place he said:

> Whoso, O monkey-king, like you, combines
> Truth, foresight, fixed resolve, and fearlessness,
> Shall see his routed foemen turn and flee.

And then the crocodile went to his own dwelling-place.

The Master identified the birth: Devadatta was the crocodile, the crocodile's wife was a young and beautiful female ascetic who was used by the Buddha's enemies to cause trouble, and " I myself was the monkey-king ".

[1] This, by the way, is said not to be a fact. But perhaps this crocodile did !

THE MONKEYS AND THE WATER-OGRE

ONCE on a pilgrimage the Buddha and his Brotherhood came
to a lake around which canes were growing. When the canes
were picked it was discovered that, unlike most canes, they
were straight and hollow. They asked the Buddha why this
was so, and he told them the following story.

Once the life that was to become the Buddha took birth as
a monkey, king of eighty thousand monkeys who lived in a
large forest. The forest was so large that they often found
themselves in unfamiliar parts with fruit they were not used to
and lakes they did not know. Their king therefore told them
never to eat an unknown fruit or drink from any pond or lake
without first asking him, for some of the fruit was poisonous
and some of the lakes were the homes of water-ogres or demons.

One day the thirsty monkeys came to a lake, and asked their
leader for permission to drink. Before he gave it he went
to the lake himself. He saw round it many footprints of animals
going towards it, but none of the footprints were coming away
from it. He therefore reasoned that the lake must have a
water-ogre in it who ate the unwary drinkers. So he told the
monkeys to wait.

After a time the water-ogre was tired of waiting for the
hundreds of monkeys to come and drink and she came out to
them. Her form was horrible—blue belly, white face, red
hands and feet. She asked them why they did not go down to
drink, and they in turn asked her if it was not true that she ate
all those who went to drink? She agreed that it was and told
them that she would eat them too.

Meanwhile the king-monkey was thinking of a plan, and he told the ogre that they *would* drink but she would not eat them.

Taking a cane which was growing on the bank he blew into it, holding the thought of the Ten Perfections [1] in his mind so strongly that it became an Act of Truth. The cane became straight and hollow inside. By a similar Act of Faith he said that all the canes round the lake should be hollow and straight, and immediately they became so. Then he told the monkeys to take a cane each, put it into the water and drink through it.

This they did and the water-ogre could not catch them.

Since that time all the canes that grow round this lake are hollow and straight, and so will they be until the end of this great period of time in which we live, for this is one of the four great miracles of our age.

The Buddha identified the birth. Devadatta was the water-ogre. " I myself was the king-monkey."

[1] Ten Perfections: Charity, Morality, Renunciation, Wisdom, Energy, Forbearance, Truthfulness, Resolution, Kindness, Equanimity.

NANDRIYA THE MONKEY-KING

ONE day the Brothers were discussing Devadatta, his cruelty, harshness and tyrannical methods. Also his plans to kill the Buddha.

When the Master came and asked what they had been discussing and they told him, he replied that this was not the first birth in which Devadatta had been cruel and harsh. And he told them the following story.

Once the life that was to become the Buddha took form as a monkey and ruled over eighty thousand monkeys. His name was Nandriya, a word meaning jolly. He lived in the Himalayas with his younger brother, Jollikins, and his blind mother.

Every day he left his mother and went to find fruit for food, always sending some back to her. Even so, she got thinner and thinner, and one day when she seemed almost on the point of dying he asked her why this was since she had plenty of fruit to eat. Then he learnt that the fruit had never reached her.

Knowing how important the relationship of mother and son really is, he decided to give the leadership of the monkeys to his brother and take his mother away from the herd and look after her himself. His brother, however, refused to accept the leadership and said he would go with them. They settled happily together in a banyan tree some distance away and every day the sons gathered fruit and fed their mother.

For some time all was well, but one day a young Brahmin came that way and saw them. This man was evil in character and though he had been taught at the famous university of Takkasila he had now fallen to the position where he made what living he could for himself and his wife and family by catching and selling any animals he could find in the forest.

As a young man he had been educated by a famous tutor at the university, but when the time came for him to leave, the tutor had told him he was cruel and violent, and, he added, such people never prospered in life but came to grief in the end. Leaving the university the young Brahmin went to Benares and married, but he could not earn his living there and went to the small village near the forest where he now lived. It was when he was returning home one day empty-handed that he saw the banyan tree, and thinking there might be something there for him went towards it. There he saw the mother monkey. The sons had just fed her and were now sitting behind her out of sight of the man, but they could see him. As he got ready to kill the mother monkey Nandriya called out to him that she was no good, being only an old monkey, and if he would save her he could take him, Nandriya, instead. The man agreed and killed Nandriya. Then he aimed at the mother monkey again. This time Jollikins called out to him saying if he would spare the mother he would allow himself to be shot. The man agreed, but when he had shot Jollikins also he shot the mother. Then he fastened all three to a bamboo stick and started for his home.

At that very moment, though he was unaware of the fact, a thunderbolt fell on his home and burnt it to the ground, together with his wife and two children. All that remained were the roof and a bamboo stick which kept it in place.

When the man was nearly home he met a friend who told him what had happened, and in his fear and anxiety he dropped the bamboo stick on which the monkeys were and ran towards his home.

As he entered what had been his house the bamboo stick

supporting the roof broke and fell on his head and killed him; the earth opened in front of him and it seemed as if the flames of hell itself rose up and swallowed him. As he disappeared he remembered the warning given him by his former tutor:

I call to mind my teacher's words; so this is what he meant !
Be careful you should nothing do of which you might repent.

Whatever a man does, the same he in himself will find;
The good man good; and evil he that evil has designed;
And so our deeds are all like seeds, and bring forth fruit in kind.

The Buddha identified the birth: Devadatta was the hunter, Sariputta the tutor, Ananda Jollikins, and " I myself was Nandriya ".

THE GREAT-HEARTED MONKEY

THIS story was told when the Brothers had been discussing the good deeds done by the Tathagata [1] towards relations.

The Buddha explained that this was not the first time he had done such deeds.

Once the life that was to become the Buddha took form as a giant monkey, leader of eighty thousand monkeys who lived near a mango tree on the bank of the Ganges.

When the fruit on the tree was ripe it fell either on to dry ground, under the tree itself, or, from one branch which spread out over the Ganges, into the water.

The king-monkey thought one day when the fruit was ripe and fell into the water trouble to them could arise, for it might be carried away and found. Therefore he told the herd to eat the flowers or fruit on that branch before it was ripe and ready to fall. This they did and lived in safety for many years.

Unfortunately one day an ants' nest hid just one fruit which, when it was ripe, fell into the Ganges and was carried away.

Some days later the king was bathing in the Ganges. As was the custom at that time a net was placed below him in the water and another one above him, and when he left the water his servants found the mango fruit caught in the upper net. Not knowing what fruit it was they took it to him. He, also, had never seen such a fruit before and enquiries were made to find out what it was. Finally a forester told the king that it was a mango fruit and good to eat. The king then cut it, gave part to the forester, ate some himself and gave the rest to his followers.

[1] A title of the Buddha.

It tasted so delicious that he asked where more like it could be found and the forester told him that it came from a tree which grew in the Himalayas on a river-bank.

The king then ordered that a train of boats should go up the river (since the mango fruit had been carried down) until they reached the tree, and he himself and his courtiers went on the journey. It is not known how long they took, but in time they reached the place and they all had a good meal of mangoes and then settled down under the tree for the night, with guards set and lighted fires around.

The king however did not sleep. In the night he heard the monkeys come down to the tree and he ordered that his soldiers should bring their arrows and shoot them so that they could all eat monkey flesh the next day. But when the monkeys saw the tree surrounded by men they went hastily back to their king and told him. And he said he would find a way to save them.

Then he climbed up a branch of a tree which rose straight up into the air, and when he reached a great height he went along a bough which had grown towards the river. From the end of this he leapt to the other bank. Calculating the length of his leap he broke a bamboo shoot of the appropriate length, stripped it of leaves, joined a part of it to a tree, calculated how much would be left free in the air, and bound the other end to his waist. Then he sprang back towards his home.

But he had miscalculated, for he had forgotten the piece of bamboo which was tied to his waist, and he was only just able to reach an outflung branch which stretched out towards him. This he grasped firmly in his hand and, calling to the monkeys, he told them to tread swiftly and lightly on his back and down the bamboo branch to safety.

One by one the monkeys saluted him and crossed over to

the other bank, asking his forgiveness for thus treading on him. All but one. He was an evil one and thought to himself that now he could harm the monkey king ! So he climbed up to a high branch and jumped with all the force he had, straight on to the middle of the tired, stretched-out back. The force broke the king-monkey's heart and he was in great pain.

All this the king had watched, and he wondered that an animal had been clever enough to think out this plan. He decided to do what he could to help so brave an animal, and ordering his men to take the boats towards it he had it brought down gently and placed on an oiled hide on a platform he had had built. There the poor monkey was bathed, rubbed with oil and clothed in clean yellow cloth.

As he rested, the king spoke to him and asked why he had done so brave a thing:

You made yourself a bridge for them to pass in safety through:
What are you to them then, monkey, and what are they to you ?

The dying monkey answered: " Victorious king, I guard the herd, I am their lord and chief," and he told him all that had happened when " they were filled with fear of thee and stricken sore with grief ". He said:

Therefore I fear no pain of death, bonds do not give me pain,
The happiness of those was won o'er whom I used to reign.

A parable for thee, O king, if thou the truth wouldst read:
The happiness of kingdom and of army and of steed
And city must be dear to thee, if thou wouldst rule indeed.

Very soon the monkey died and the king ordered that all honour should be paid to him as though he were a king. Where his body was cremated the king erected a shrine in which lamps were kept alight and flowers and incense offered. He took the skull and had it inlaid with gold and placed on the point of a spear in front of a shrine. All the people paid homage to so brave an animal. Later the skull was taken to Benares and honoured for seven days, after which it was kept in a shrine.

Ever after the king took the good teaching of the monkey-king to heart, gave alms and performed other good deeds, and ruling his kingdom righteously in all ways he went to heaven when he died.

The Buddha identified the birth: The monkey herd was the present Assembly, Ananda the king, " I myself was the monkey-king."

THE SIXTY-YEAR-OLD ELEPHANT

ON another day the Brothers discussed Devadatta, saying that he was devoid of pity, and when the Master heard of the discussion he said not only now but in former times he was pitiless. And he told the following story.

Once the life that was to become the Buddha took birth as an elephant and became the leader of eighty thousand elephants in the Himalayas.

One day when he was sixty years of age a mother quail laid her eggs in the feeding-ground of the elephants, and in time the little quails broke the shells and came out. But before their wings had grown and they could fly, the elephants came to the spot. Terrified for her little ones, the mother quail went to the leader elephant and said:

> Elephant of sixty years,
> Forest lord amongst thy peers,
> I am but a puny bird,
> Thou a leader of the herd;
> With my wings I homage pay,
> Spare my little ones, I pray.

The elephant leader told her not to fear for he would spare them, and to save them from the herd he stood over them until all the elephants had passed by. Save one, a rogue elephant who would not obey his command. Before he left he told the mother quail and advised her to speak to the rogue herself.

When the rogue elephant appeared the mother quail beseeched him to spare her little ones, but he told her:

> I will slay thy young ones, quail;
> What can thy poor help avail?
> My left foot can crush with ease
> Many thousand birds like these.

And placing his foot on them he crushed them to death and swept the remains away so that no trace of them was left.

The mother quail sat on a tree and watched, and thought:

> Power abused is not all gain,
> Power is often folly's bane,
> Beast that didst my young ones kill,
> I will work thee mischief still.

And she made her plans.

First she made friends with a crow by doing him a good deed, and when the crow asked what it could do in return, she asked him to peck out the eyes of the rogue elephant. This he did.

Then she made friends with a blue fly, and when the fly asked what it could do for her, she told it to lay its eggs in the rogue elephant's eye sockets. This it did.

Then she did a good deed for a frog, and when it asked what it could do in return, she told it to go down to the bottom of a cliff and croak.

Soon, the rogue elephant, maddened by pain and thirst heard the frog and immediately thought there was water. Hastily he went towards it and fell over the cliff and was killed.

> A quail with crow, blue fly and frog allied
> Once proved the issue of a deadly feud.
> Through them King elephant untimely died:
> Therefore all quarrelling should be eschewed.

The Master added, " Brethren, one should not incur the

hostility of anyone. These four combined, weak as they were, destroyed the elephant."

He identified the birth: Devadatta was the rogue elephant. "I myself was the elephant leader."

THE WHITE ELEPHANT

ONE day the Brethren were discussing the ingratitude of Deva-datta, and when the Buddha came he asked them what they were discussing. They told him and he said that it was not the first time, for he had never known my virtues. And he told the following story.

Once the life that was to become the Buddha was born as a white elephant. He lived in the Himalayas and became the leader of eighty thousand elephants. His eyes were clear and sparkled like diamonds, his mouth was red and healthy, his trunk like a silver rope flecked with red gold, and his feet were as though made of polished lacquer.

One day he became aware that all was not well with the herd, for evil had crept in; some of them had lost their natural instincts and were misbehaving. As he could not do anything about it he left them and went to live alone in another part of the forest.

Some time later he saw a forester weeping for he had lost his way, and he thought he would help him. But every time he moved towards him the poor man ran further away. See-ing this, the elephant stood still and made the man realize that he meant him no harm. Then the man told him he had lost his way, and the elephant said he would take him and put him on the right path, but he warned him not to let anyone know in what part of the forest he had seen him. " Tell no man of my abode."

But the man noted all the markings of the way out.

One day a little later some ivory workers made it known

that they wanted living ivory, *i.e.* ivory from a living elephant, and the man went back to the forest and told the elephant that he could not support himself at his work. He begged that he would let him have a piece of his tusks.

The elephant said he could cut off one whole tusk, and he bent his knees so that the man could reach him. But the man cut off the greater part of both tusks, and returning home, sold them.

In a short time he had spent the money and he returned to the elephant asking for more ivory. This he was granted. He returned home, spent the money and went again to the forest. This time he asked if he could have the stumps of the tusks.

The elephant did not refuse but lay down, and the man climbed up his silver trunk, and, kicking away at the roots of the tusks till he had cleared away the flesh, sawed out the stumps and taking them with him went away.

But at this last dastardly act the earth herself shook as though she were unable to bear any longer this wickedness. A yawning chasm appeared in front of the man and he disappeared within.

All this was seen by a Tree Sprite who said:

> Ingratitude lacks more: the more it gets;
> Not all the world can glut its appetite.

Henceforth, the elephant lived on in peace.

The Master identified the birth: Devadatta was the hunter, I myself the good king elephant, Sariputta the Tree Sprite.

THE SIX-TUSKER

THIS story was told of a woman ascetic of good family who went one day to hear the Buddha speak.

She wondered to herself whether she had ever served any of his family in any life. Perhaps she had once been his wife? Then came the thought, few wives are good, many are ill-disposed, and she wondered if she had been. And she laughed to herself. But soon the remembrance of what she had done in a past life came to her and she saw how she had sent a hunter to destroy him and she wept.

The Master smiled and told this story.

Once the life that was to become the Buddha took form as a white elephant and ruled over a herd of eight thousand elephants. His tusks were magnificent and seemed to radiate six different colours, this fact giving him the name Six(rayed) Tusker; his forehead was massive and his trunk like a silver rope. He had two wives, Mahasubhadda or Subhadda Major, and Chullasubhadda, or Subhadda Minor.

He lived near the Six-Tusker Lake in the Himalayan mountains and life was good. This lake was set in beautiful surroundings and was beautiful in itself for it was covered with lotus blooms of many colours. Round it, in ever-widening circles, were fruit trees, rice fields, more trees, a bamboo wood and seven great mountain ranges. North-east of the lake was a magnificent banyan tree which gave shade to the elephants in the summer, and to the west there was a golden cave in which they could shelter when the monsoon rains poured down through the mountains. The elephants lived a happy life, playing among the fruit trees or in the cool refreshing water.

One day when the trees were in full bloom he was playing with his wives among them and he struck one tree with his forehead. Masses of flowers and green leaves fell down on Mahasubhadda—but Chullasubhadda was covered with red ants and dead leaves which had also been dislodged, for she was on the other side of her husband, and for a moment she felt jealous.

On another day the Six-Tusker and his wives went to bathe in the lake and were scrubbed down by the other elephants. When they rested, the herd went in to bathe and threw flowers to them. One elephant found a seven-headed lotus blossom and gave it to the king. He received it graciously, shook some of the pollen on his forehead and then passed it to Mahasubhadda. Once again Chullasubhadda was jealous, and this time vowed vengeance.

Some time later a band of wise beings visited the Six-Tusker and he offered them fruit and flowers. Chullasubhadda did the same, but she added a silent prayer that she might be born a princess, marry the king of Benares and bring about the death of the Six-Tusker. Taking this resolve she refused food and died.

In time she was born as a beautiful princess and did in fact become the favourite wife of the king of Benares.

One day she remembered her resolve, and pretending to be ill, retired to her bed. When the king asked what was the matter, she told him she had a very strong unsatisfied desire, and unless this could be fulfilled she would die. In his anxiety he promised her that whatever she desired he would obtain for her, however difficult it might be. But when he asked what the desire was she would not tell him. Instead she asked if all the hunters in the kingdom could come to her and they were

sent for. When they came she told them that she had had a
dream in which she was shown a glorious six-tusker elephant,
and unless she could possess the tusks she would die. Looking
at the hunters she chose the most uncouth and cruel-looking one
and demanded that he should get them for her.

At first the man was afraid, but when she explained that in
the dream she did get the tusks, he was satisfied and asked where
the elephant was to be found.

> Not far this bathing-place of his,
> A deep and goodly pool it is:
> There bees do swarm and flowers abound,
> And there this royal beast is found.
>
> Now lotus-crowned, fresh from his bath
> He gladly takes his homeward path,
> As lily-white and tall he moves
> Behind the queen he fondly loves.

And he agreed to go. She sent him away for a week, while
she prepared for his journey.

After seven days he returned and was given his instructions
and the various things which had been provided for the journey
—food, ropes, a grappling iron, an iron staff, a leather umbrella
and a leather bag in which to carry them. Putting them all in
the bag he slung it on his back in such a way that both hands
were free, and, in a chariot, watched by the king and queen
and followed by a huge crowd, he started on the journey.

It took him seven years, seven months and seven days to
reach the great banyan tree where the Six-Tusker was living
at peace. His journey had been difficult and he had needed all
the tackle the queen had provided. He felled trees, dug paths,
crossed marshes and climbed mountains. Once he used his
umbrella as a kind of parachute. Tying his rope to the top of

the mountain, with the bag at the other end of the rope, he got into the bag and opened his umbrella. The wind caught it and prevented his too swift descent.

When, at last, he reached the banyan tree near to the place where the Six-Tusker bathed, he dug a pit, covered it lightly with wood planks and threw the loose soil he had dug up over them. Then, dressing himself in the yellow robe of a hermit —which would save him from death since hermits could not be killed—he got into the hole, pointed his arrow through a gap in the loose soil, and waited.

Soon, all unsuspecting, the Six-Tusker came along to bathe. The poisoned arrow was shot. And, with a great cry of pain and anger, the elephant moved towards the hunter to kill him. He was stayed by the sight of the yellow robe and said:

> Whoso is marred with sinful taint
> And void of truth and self-restraint,
> Though robed in yellow he may be,
> No claim to sanctity has he.

He asked the man why he had done this thing. Was it, he asked, by his own wish or was he obeying the orders of another?

Then the man told him everything. Full of compassion, the Six-Tusker said he would let him take his tusks to the queen, but, he pointed out, she did not really want them; what she wanted was a sign that he had been killed.

To help the hunter he lay down so that he could climb up his great shining head to the massive forehead, and once there the hunter put his knee in the unresponsive mouth and began to hack through the flesh to the roots of the tusks. He was so clumsy that at last the Six-Tusker could stand the pain no longer. He asked the man to lift up his trunk for him for he was too weak to do it himself. Then, with the knife in it, placed there by the hunter, the elephant began to cut away his own tusks. When they were free he gave them to the man.

He also gave him the magic power by which he could return to the queen in seven days instead of taking the seven years he had needed to come. With this last gift the great elephant died.

When Subhadda and the other elephants saw that the hunter had left they went to their leader. Finding that he was dead, a great fire was made and two young strong elephants reverently lifted the great body with their tusks and placed it in the midst of the fire so that it was reduced to ashes. Then, with Subhadda at their head, they sorrowfully returned to their dwelling-place.

In seven days' time the hunter returned to the queen and presented her with the tusks, telling her that he had fulfilled her command and killed the elephant.

She took the large and lovely tusks on her lap and looked at them for some time. And as she looked, the memory of the majesty and kindliness of her former husband came back to her mind, and remorse and grief so filled her heart that she died.

The Buddha identified the birth:

> " The wretch who took those tusks so white,
> Unmatched on earth, so shining bright,
> And brought them to Benares town
> Is now as Devadatta known ! "

> " She whom you used to see," he said,
> " A yellow-robed ascetic maid,
> Was erst a queen and I," he cried,
> " Was that king elephant who died."

THE GOLDEN CRAB

THIS story was told about a landowner of the Buddha's time who, when travelling with his wife to collect his debts, was taken by robbers. The chief robber thought of killing him so that he could possess his wife, but she told him that she would never be his; if he killed her husband she would kill herself. The robber consequently let them go.

On their way home they called to pay homage to the Buddha. When he asked them where they had been they told him the story, and he said that it was not only in this existence that the woman had saved someone's life. In the past she had saved the lives of others. Then, at their request, he told them the following story.

Once the life that was to become the Buddha took form as an elephant, son of a king-elephant who lived near a lake in the Himalayas. In the lake lived a large golden crab who ate elephant flesh. Every time the elephants went to bathe or drink in the lake he caught one of them and ate it, for he was more powerful even than an elephant. When, therefore, the queen elephant was about to give birth to her son she went to another mountain where the young one could be brought up more safely. In due time the young elephant was born and grew up to a great size. He was so beautiful that his body looked like a purple mountain. He married a beautiful she-elephant.

As he grew older he thought of his father and the crab, and with his mother and his wife went to ask if he could be allowed to try and defeat the crab. At first his father refused for he did not think it could be done, but at last he gave permission.

The young elephant then called the herd together and asked whether the crab caught them as they went to bathe, while bathing, or when getting ready to leave. He was told the catch was made as they left. So he told them to go as usual to bathe and he would go with them, and when it was time to leave he would leave last.

Accordingly they went, and having finished their bathe began to leave. But just as the young elephant was leaving, the crab caught his foot in his cruel claws and he could not move.

His wife had left with the others, but when she saw he was caught he called out to her:

> Gold-clawed creature with projecting eyes,
> Tarn-bred, hairless, clad in bony shell,
> He has caught me ! hear my woeful cries.

And she immediately returned to comfort him.

Try as he would he could not free himself; neither could he drag the crab, but, instead, the crab began to drag him towards the lake. Trying to comfort him his wife sang:

> Leave you ? never ! never will I go—
> Noble husband, with your years threescore,
> All four quarters of the earth can show
> None so dear as thou hast been of yore.

As the crab slowly dragged the elephant she turned to him and began to praise him:

> Of all the crabs that in the sea,
> Ganges, or Nerbudda be,
> You are best and chief, I know:
> Hear me—let my husband go !

Her voice infatuated the crab and he loosened his grip. Immediately the elephant stamped on him. Then he cried aloud the cry of triumph and the herd returned, fell on the crab and stamped it to dust.

All but the two claws. These had somehow been flung away from the body and were left there. In the rainy season the waters of the lake covered them, and when the dry season began and the waters receded, they were carried down the Ganges. Here one of them was found by the ten brothers of the king and turned into a drum called Anaka. The other reached the sea and was found by evil demons who turned it into a drum called Alambara. Later on the demons were defeated by the Great Spirit and the drum was taken for his own. So people today say "Thundering like the Alambara-cloud".

The Master identified the birth: The wife was the she-elephant, "I myself was her mate."

THE OBEDIENT ELEPHANT

The Brethren were one day discussing how Devadatta was infuriated by the perfection of the Buddha.

When the Master came to them he asked what they had been discussing and when he heard he said that in former times, as well as now, Devadatta was maddened by his perfections, and he told the following story.

Once the life that was to become the Buddha took birth as ꞁ elephant. He was white all over, and so beautiful in every way that he was made the king's state elephant.

One day, a feast day, the king rode on the magnificently robed elephant through the decorated city, the streets lined with great crowds of people. Usually on these occasions the crowd was enthusiastic in its praise of the king, but on this day they all sang the praises of the elephant. They spoke of its beauty, of its magnificence, of its wonderful gait, of its beautifully proportioned body, and so on. All this the king heard and he was jealous. He determined that the elephant must die.

Calling to the mahout he asked if the elephant was very well trained, and hearing that he was, he got down and ordered that the mahout should take the elephant up to the summit of a mountain. He, with his courtiers, followed behind.

When they arrived the king told the mahout to lead the elephant to the edge of the precipice. This was done. Then the king ordered that it should stand on three legs. The elephant obeyed the command of the mahout. The king ordered that it should now stand on two fore legs, then on the two hind legs. All this was done. Lastly the king said that if it was so well trained as it was supposed to be it should now stand in the air.

Now, without doubt, the mahout realized that the king wanted to kill the elephant and bending down so that he could whisper, he told the elephant what the king wanted. He asked it whether it had the power to fly in the air, and if it had it should do so and take him to the king of Benares who would be a better master.

Then the elephant rose in the air, and before he flew off the mahout told the king that this elephant was too good for him and would seek a more worthy master.

Soon the elephant and mahout arrived at Benares and the elephant halted in the air above the king's courtyard, much to the surprise of the king's men who rushed to tell their master of the strange sight. When the king came, the elephant descended and the mahout told him why they had come.

The king told them they could certainly stay with him and he ordered the city to be decorated and the elephant taken round to the State stables. He then divided his kingdom into three parts: the mahout was to have one part, the elephant another, and he himself the third part.

His power grew so much that he became Emperor of all India.

The Master identified the birth: Devadatta was the king who owned the elephant, Ananda was the mahout, Sariputta the king of Benares, and " I myself was the elephant".

GRANNIE'S BLACKIE

THIS story was told by the Buddha when he heard the Brothers describing his perfections.

Once the life that was to become the Buddha took form as a black bull which, while still young, was given to a widow in payment of a debt. She brought him up with great care, feeding him on rice and treating him as though he were her own son; and he grew up into a fine animal, black as jet, strong, and yet kind and gentle. Children loved him for he would let them play with his tail, catch him by the horns and ride on his back.

One day he thought he ought to try and repay the widow for all she had done for him and he began to look for some work he could do.

It happened just at this time that a merchant with fifty wagons came that way and in order to continue his journey had to ford a river. But when the oxen tried to take the wagons across they found the ground so uneven and rough that they had to give up. Even though fifty oxen were yoked to one wagon it was impossible to pass on.

In this difficulty the merchant looked about for help, and seeing among some cattle grazing near the magnificent form of the black bull, asked some men to whom it belonged. When he heard that the bull had no master he tried to get him to move towards the wagons, thinking that he would use his strength without having to pay any owner.

But Blackie, as the Black Bull had been nicknamed, would not move. Somehow he made the man understand that he

86

wanted payment for his services, and the merchant offered him two coins for each wagon he took across. Then, indeed, Blackie moved forward and after making great efforts, and becoming very tired in the process, he got all the wagons across. Standing at the head of the caravan he waited for payment.

The merchant put coins in a bag and hung the bag round Blackie's neck. But the bull did not move, and until he did the caravan could not pass on. Again he made the merchant understand that he had only put one coin per wagon in the bag and not two as he had promised! So the merchant added one coin more for each wagon and Blackie moved away, the caravan went on and Blackie ran home to tell the widow what had happened.

When the widow saw how tired he was she told him he need never think of repaying her for what she had done for it had given her great pleasure to do it, but she was, as she made him understand, very grateful for his kind thought.

> With heavy loads to carry, with bad roads,
> They harness "Blackie"; *he* soon draws the load.

The Buddha identified the birth: "I myself was the bull."

GOBLIN TOWN

THIS story was told by the Buddha when he heard that a Brother in his Order had become a backslider. Asked for the reason, the Brother said that his passion had taken hold of him because he had seen a well-dressed woman. The Master said that these women tempt men by their voice, figure, touch, wiles, scent, etc., and men fell into their grasp, ruined their characters, lost their wealth and everything.

" Those who neglect the advice of the Buddhas come to great misery; those who abide by it come to happiness."

And he told the following story.

Once the life that was to become the Buddha took form as a white horse with a head like a bird and a mane like flowing grass. He had the magic power of flying through the air and was therefore called the Cloud-horse.

Now at the south of India is an island off which in olden times many ships were wrecked, and the women of the island dressed in their best, used to meet the shipwrecked sailors, give them food and ask them to be their husbands. These women were evil demons, Yakkhinis, and they had the power to call up illusive pictures of prosperous fertile lands and beautiful surroundings, so that the men often went home with them. They did not know that though they would be fêted for a time, when another ship was wrecked the women would put them in dungeons, kill them and eat them while the new sailors took their places.

One day some merchants were shipwrecked and as usual went home with the women. In the night the chief Yakkhini left the leader whom she had chosen for her own husband, and went to the dungeons, killed and ate a sailor and returned home. The leader realized that something was wrong and suddenly the truth flashed upon him.

In the morning he told the others that these women were man-eating demons, and half of them decided to leave the place and hide. But the other half decided to stay.

Just at this time the Cloud-horse was flying from the Himalayas across India to Ceylon, and as he went he called out to any who could hear: "Does anyone want to go home?" When the leader and the others heard and saw him they were delighted and said they certainly wanted to go home. So the horse came down to them, some climbed on his back, others seized his tail and some he gathered up himself, and flew away with them all to their own land. When he saw them safely settled he flew off again.

Said the Buddha:

They who will neglect the Buddha when he tells them what to do,
As the goblins ate the merchants, likewise they shall perish too.

They who hearken to the Buddha when he tells them what to do,
As the bird-horse saved the merchants, they shall win salvation too.

He identified the birth—he was the horse, the two hundred and fifty men who went with him were his present followers. The backsliding brother then entered on the Path.

THE PARIAH DOG

THIS story was told to show how one should act for the good of one's family.

Once the life that was to become the Buddha took form as a pariah dog, a dog with no home. He lived in the cemetery of the king's city and got what food he could from garbage. Owing to his character he soon became the leader of all the other pariah dogs of the city.

One day the king went out in his chariot, drawn by milk-white horses, and after enjoying himself all day returned as the sun went down. As it was late the horses were taken out of harness and housed, but the harness was left lying in the court-yard. Unfortunately it rained during the night and the harness go so wet that the leather parts became soft and sodden, and when the king's dogs ran into the courtyard they tore it to pieces and ate them.

When morning came the servants saw what had happened and told the king that the pariah dogs had entered the courtyard through the sewers and eaten the royal harness. The king therefore issued an order that all the pariah dogs in the city should be destroyed.

The news reached the dogs and they rushed to the cemetery and, trembling with fear, told their leader. But he calmed them and told them not to worry; somehow he would save them. After pondering for some time he thought of a plan, and telling them to wait for him he started out for the palace. As he passed through the streets he repeated to himself all the time, " Let no hand be lifted to throw stick or stone at me," and so concentrated was he in this thought that no one did throw anything at him and he reached the palace unmolested. Such is the power of the Truth-Act, or Act of Faith.

Arriving at the palace he passed through the gates and finally arrived at the door of the Council Chamber where the king was already seated on his throne, receiving complaints or listening to the wishes of his subjects. Hastily rushing into the Chamber he took refuge under the royal throne.

The king asked him what his trouble was, and he asked the king if it was true that he had ordered all the pariah dogs of the city to be destroyed. The king admitted that it was true. Then, said the dog:

> The dogs that in the royal palace grow,
> The well-bred dogs, so strong and fair of form,—
> Not these, but only we, are doomed to die.
> Here's no impartial sentence meted out
> To all alike; 'tis slaughter of the poor.

But, the king said, the reason for the order was that the dogs had eaten the royal harness. This could not be, said the dog, for no pariah dog could get into the courtyard ! If that was so, replied the king, who could have eaten the harness ? Then the dog told the king that it was the royal dogs who were the culprits and he could prove it. Being a just king he asked for proof, and the dog asked that all the royal dogs should be brought into the Chamber and be given a meal of kusa grass and buttermilk. This was done.

Then, as the people watched, the royal dogs became sick and vomited pieces of leather !

The king was so pleased with the wisdom of the pariah dog that he said he would withdraw his order and instead, he ordered that henceforth all pariah dogs should be fed on the same food as he himself ate. The pariah dog was pleased, but he asked if the king would also spare the lives of all other living things. This also the king agreed to do and ever after refrained from killing any living creature, living long and ruling wisely.

The Buddha identified the birth, Ananda was the king and " I myself was the dog ".

THE JUJUBE FRUIT

ONE day it became known that the king of Kosala and his queen had quarrelled, and the king would have nothing to do with her. The Buddha knew of this and went to the palace with five hundred of his followers. He was welcomed by the king and food was prepared for them all. Before eating, the Buddha asked where the queen was. The king told him that she had become intoxicated with all the honour bestowed on her. Then the Master told him that he had given her the honour himself and therefore he ought not to take it away again and get rid of her, but rather forgive whatever offence she had done to him.

The king relented and sent for the queen, who attended on the Master. He told them both that they should live together in peace, and having spoken of the blessings of friendship he went on his way.

Later the Brethren discussed the incident, and when the Master had asked what their discussion had been about, he told them that not for the first time had he settled their disputes. And he told them the following story.

Once a king looked through a window and saw a girl with a basket of jujube fruit on her head. She was calling out, " Jujubes, ripe jujubes, who'll buy my jujubes ? " and her voice was so lovely that he fell in love with her. She was brought to him and he made her his chief queen.

For some time they lived happily together for the king was very fond of her, but one day when he was with her and eating jujube fruit from a gold plate she asked him:

What is this egg-shaped fruit, my lord, so pretty and red of hue,
In a gold dish set before thee ? Pray tell me, where they grew.

At this the king was angry and asked her why she did not recognize the fruit for:

Bare-headed and meanly clad, my queen, thou once didst feel no
　　shame,
To fill thy lap with the jujube fruit, and now thou dost ask its name;
Thou art eaten up with pride, my queen, thou findest no pleasure
　　in life,
Begone and gather thy jujubes again. Thou shalt be no longer
　　my wife.

In that birth the Master was the king's minister and he thought that he alone could reconcile the two and prevent the king from turning the queen away, so he told the king:

These are the sins of a woman, my lord, promoted to high estate:
Forgive her and cease from thine anger, O King, for 'twas thou
　　didst make her great.

The king then forgave her and restored her to her position. Afterwards they lived amicably together.

The Master identified the birth: The king of Kosala was the king, the queen was the jujube queen, and " I myself was the Minister".

THE SAD FAIRIES

ONE day the king of Benares and his queen quarrelled and the king was angry and would not look at his queen.

And the queen wondered if the Buddha knew of this.

The Buddha did hear of it and on the following day went to Benares, and having sought alms, went to the gate of the palace with his Brethren. The king went out to meet him and took him, with the Brethren, to the terrace and gave them water and food. Then when they had eaten the king sat apart. The Buddha asked him why the queen was not there and he answered that it was because of her pride in her exalted state.

The Master replied, " O great king ! long, long ago when you were a fairy, you kept apart for one night from your mate, and then went mourning for seven hundred years ! " And he told the following story.

Once the king of Benares wanted to eat venison again broiled on charcoal, and gave his kingdom in the charge of the courtiers while he, with a pack of well-trained hounds, started for the Himalayas. He travelled along the Ganges until he could go no further, and then along a tributary stream, killing deer and pig whose flesh he broiled and ate. In time he reached a great height and found himself at a place where a pleasant stream ran full, sometimes breast high, in which all kinds of fish gambolled. The sand at the water's edge was fine and pure and looked like silver. The trees on both banks were full of flowers and fruit, and birds and bees flew about drunk with fruit and the honey of flowers. In the thicket herds of deer grazed.

In this idyllic spot two fairies embraced and kissed and wept.

The king wondered why they were both sad and gay at the same time and thought he would ask them. He snapped his fingers at his hounds and they crouched in the undergrowth. Then, laying aside his bow and arrows, he very quietly approached the fairies and asked them why they laughed and wept.

The fairy wife told him they had done this for seven hundred years because of one night's parting, for:

> We both apart one night had lain,
> Both loveless, full of bitter pain
>   Thinking each of each: but never
> Will that night come back again.

The king asked why they had been apart and the fairy continued:

> Shaded thick yon river flows
> Between the rocks: a storm arose:
>   Then with anxious care to find me
> Right across my loved one goes.

> All the while with busy feet
> I gathered thyme and meadowsweet
>   All to make my love a garland
> And myself, when we should meet.

> Clustering harebell, violet blue,
> And white narcissus fresh with dew,
>   All to make my love a garland
> And myself, when we should meet.

> Then I plucked a bunch of rose,
> That is the fairest flower that grows,
>   All to make my love a garland
> And myself, when we should meet.

Flowers next and leaves I found,
And strewed them thickly on the ground,
   Where the livelong night together
We might slumber soft and sound.

Sandal and sweet woods anon
I pounded small upon a stone,
   Perfume for my love's limbs making,
Sweetest perfume for my own.

By the river flowing fast
I gathered lilies to the last:
   Evening came—the river swelling
Made it hopeless to get past.

There we stood on either shore,
Each on other gazing o'er.
   How we laughed and cried together!
Ah! that night we suffered sore.

Morning came, the sun was high
And soon we saw the river dry.
   Then we crossed, and close embracing
Both at once we laugh and cry.

Seven hundred years but three
Since we were parted, I and he.
   When two loving hearts are severed
Seems a whole long life to be.

The king asked them then how old they were! And the fairy
wife answered:

      A thousand summers strong, and hale,
      Never deadly pains assail,
         Little sorrow, bliss abundant,
      To the end love's joys prevail.

The Buddha added that learning this lesson from the fairies the king returned to his kingdom, did not hunt any more, looked after the needy and ruled well. And he added:

> Take a lesson from the fays;
> And quarrel not, but mend your ways.
>   Lest you suffer, like the fairy,
> Your own error all your days.

> Take a lesson from the fays:
> And bicker not, but mend your ways.
>   Lest you suffer, like the fairy,
> Your own error all your days.

At the end of the story the queen approached the Buddha with reverence, saying:

> Holy man, with willing mind
> I hear thy words so good and kind.
>   Blessings on thee ! thou hast spoken,
> All my sorrow's left behind.

The quarrel was now made up and afterwards the king and queen lived happily together.

The Buddha identified the birth: The king was the fairy, the queen his wife, and " I myself was the hunter king ".

THE BRAHMIN YOUTH

ONE day the Brothers discussed together and asked whether Ananda had ever given his life for the Buddha.

The Buddha replied that he had done so in former lives, and told the following story.

Once the Buddha-to-be was born as the son of a Brahmin farmer and when he was a young man he went every day with the men to the fields.

Once when it was ploughing time he took the men to the field and then went to wash in a pool of clean water nearby.

In the pool was a small golden crab. He picked it up, put it in his outer garment and carried it with him all day. At nightfall he took it back to the pool.

This happened many days and a friendship grew up between the two.

In a corner of the field in which the youth worked there was a palm tree in which a crow and his wife lived. She often watched the young man at work and seeing that his eyes were particularly beautiful she had a great longing to eat them. So one day she told her husband, but he said he could not take them for her.

The she-crow said she knew quite well that he himself could not take them but if he would make friends with a black snake that lived in an anthill nearby he could ask him to bite the youth. Then, when the boy had fallen to the ground through the effect of the snake poison the crow could take out his eyes.

So a friendship was struck up between the crow and the snake and one day the snake asked what he could do for the crow. The crow asked him to bite the youth.

The next day the youth as usual washed in the pool and took the golden crab back with him to the field. But, suddenly, the snake, hidden from sight, bit him in the leg and he fell to the ground. The crow flew up at once to get the eyes and the snake fled to the anthill. While the crow was trying to get the eyes the crab came out of the youth's clothes and caught him in his claws. The crow cried out for help and the snake came towards them with its hood up ready to strike again. But the crab caught it too and held it fast.

The snake, finding out why the crab had caught him, asked him to free them and he would draw the poison from the youth. The crab therefore let the snake go, but kept the crow fast in his claws as a hostage till the snake had drawn off the poison and the youth was well again. When this happened it killed both snake and crow, and the she-crow, seeing what had happened, flew away to another place.

The Master identified the birth: Mara was the serpent, Devadatta the crow, good Ananda was the crab, and " I was the Brahmin long ago".

THE MOUSE AND THE CATS

THERE was in the Brotherhood a lay sister who was known as Kana's mother. She had a daughter who was married to a man of the same caste but who lived in another village. One day the daughter visited her mother and stayed for a few days. When she did not return her husband sent a messenger asking her to come back. Receiving the message the girl asked her mother if she ought to return, and receiving an assent was prepared to go. But the mother said that as she had been away for a few days she could not go empty handed and she would make a cake for her to take.

Just when the cake was ready a Brother of the Order came for alms, and the mother gave it to him, starting to make another for the daughter.

The Brother however told another Brother and he went to the mother's dwelling just in time to receive the second cake. He told a third Brother who went in time to receive the third cake, and this Brother told another Brother who arrived in time to receive the fourth cake.

In the meantime when the wife did not return her husband sent another message. Still she did not return, for the cake she should have taken was again given away. This happened for the third time, but the third message said that if she did not return he would get another wife, which he did.

When the girl heard that he had indeed taken another wife she wept. The Master hearing this went to her mother's home and asked the reason why she wept. Having heard, he returned home.

But the Brothers talked of the matter and when the Buddha

heard they were discussing it, he said that this was not the first time that these four Brothers had taken from Kana's mother's store, and he told the following story.

Once the Buddha-to-be was born as a stone-cutter, a work at which he excelled.

Sometime before the story begins a rich merchant had hidden his vast store of money in a place known only to himself and his wife. In time the wife died, and so great was her love of money that she was reborn as a mouse and lived near the hidden store. In time the husband and then the family died, but the treasure remained hidden. Later the village was deserted and it was near this deserted village that the Buddha-to-be followed his craft.

The mouse often saw him at work and fell in love with him. One day she thought that when she died the treasure would be of no use to her, and she thought she would take a coin a day to the stone-cutter and thus share the money with him. Consequently she arrived with a coin in her mouth, and when he asked her why she brought it she said for him to buy food for her and to use the rest as he willed.

After this he bought food for her every day and used his share as he wished.

But one day the mouse was caught by a cat and begged for her life. The cat asked why he should not eat her for he was hungry. The mouse asked if the cat was hungry every day or only on that occasion, and hearing that every day the pangs of hunger attacked the cat said that if her life was spared she could bring food for him every day. This was agreed upon and every day following the mouse divided her food into halves, keeping a half for herself and giving the cat the other half.

Unfortunately on another day the mouse was caught by a

second cat and the same thing happened. Henceforth she divided her food into three portions and shared it with the two cats.

Still another cat caught her and she had to divide her food into four portions, keeping but one portion for herself. Still a further cat caught her and the same thing happened.

On this meagre diet the mouse got thinner and thinner and one day the Buddha-to-be asked her why this was since she had regular food ? Then the story came out and he blamed her for not telling him at once. Taking a piece of clear pure crystal he made a hole in it large enough to hold the mouse, and told her to get inside and look out for the cats as they came for their food. When she saw them she was to be brave and threaten all who came near her.

When the first cat came she spoke sharply to it and made it angry, the cat rushed at her to destroy her—and met the crystal wall, and died. The same thing happened to the four cats in turn. And the mouse was so grateful that after that she brought two or three coins in her mouth daily to the stone-cutter.

And for many years they lived together in friendship.

Then the Buddha said:

> Give food to one cat, Number Two appears:
> A third and fourth succeed in fruitful line;
> —Witness the four that by the crystal died.

The Master identified the birth: The four Brothers were the four cats of those days, Kana's mother was the mouse, and " I was the stone-cutter".

THE PERFUME OF THE LOTUS

ONE day a Brother of the Order went to a lotus pond and the wind carried the scent of a lotus bloom to him. A fairy of the forest rebuked him, saying that to smell the flower was a kind of theft.

The Brother returned to the monastery frightened at what he had done. When the Master saw him he asked him where he had been, and when he heard he told him it was not the first time that someone had been frightened by a goddess when smelling a flower. Even sages had been so frightened, and he told him the following story.

Once the Buddha-to-be was born in a Brahmin family and educated at Takkasila. Later on he became an ascetic and lived near a lotus pond.

One day when he was smelling a lotus bloom, a goddess spoke to him from a hollow in a tree-trunk and said:

You were never given that flower you smell, though it's only a single
    bloom;
'Tis a species of larceny reverend sir, you are stealing its perfume.

The ascetic answered her: " I neither take nor break the flower; from afar I smell the bloom."

Some time later he saw a man breaking the plants and he asked the goddess why she did not rebuke *him*? She answered:

Disgusting like a nurse's dress are men disorderly:
I have no speech with men like him, but I deign to speak to thee.
When a man is free from evil stain and seeks for purity,
A sin like a hair tip shows on him like a dark cloud in the sky.

The ascetic answered her:

Surely, fairy, you know me well, to pity me you deign;
If you ever see me do the like offence, pray speak to me again.

[But the ascetic had not yet learnt the lesson, and she rebuked him again]:

I am not here to serve you, no teaching folk are we:
Find, Brother, for yourself the path to real felicity.

The Master identified the birth: " I myself was the ascetic."

A